3 1336 00218 0330

D0090696

STORAGE

797   Kahn, R
        A season in the
sun
              895

SAN DIEGO PUBLIC LIBRARY

STORAGE

2cc
0,7

ALWAYS BRING YOUR
CARD WITH YOU.

A
Season
in the
Sun

Books by Roger Kahn

The Passionate People
The Battle for Morningside Heights
The Boys of Summer
How the Weather Was

Juvenile
Inside Big League Baseball

Edited
The World of John Lardner
The Mutual Baseball Almanac

Roger Kahn

A Season in the Sun

HARPER & ROW, PUBLISHERS

New York, Hagerstown, San Francisco, London

San Diego Public Library

Portions of this work originally appeared in somewhat different form in *Sports Illustrated.*

A SEASON IN THE SUN. Copyright © 1977 by Roger Kahn. All rights reserved. Printed in the United States of America. No part of this book may be used or reproduced in any manner whatsoever without written permission except in the case of brief quotations embodied in critical articles and reviews. For information address Harper & Row, Publishers, Inc., 10 East 53rd Street, New York, N.Y. 10022. Published simultaneously in Canada by Fitzhenry & Whiteside Limited, Toronto.

FIRST EDITION

Designed by Stephanie Krasnow

Library of Congress Cataloging in Publication Data

Kahn, Roger.
   A season in the sun.

   "Portions . . . originally appeared in Sports
illustrated."
   1. Baseball—United States. I. Title.
GV863.A1K34 1977   796.357'0973   76–26237
ISBN 0–06–012246–3

---

77 78 79 80 10 9 8 7 6 5 4 3 2 1

For Olga Kahn

student, littérateur, teacher,
who at length is learning,
in her eighth decade,
which base is second

A section of photographs follows page 114.

A
Season
in the
Sun

Prologue in Early Spring

... besides, when the sky is so blue things sing
themselves.

—E. E. CUMMINGS

Vandals had set fire to the grass. No one knew how they
had gotten wet spring grass to burn, nor why anyone
wanted to fire a soft suburban meadow, but there the ball
field lay, grimy with ash on the sixteenth day of spring.

"It's all right," the boy said. "We can play anyway."

I was wearing red sneakers, a gift Lou Brock had offered, along with a lecture on quickness and traction and
stealing bases. Brock's autograph is stitched near the in-
step and someone noticing his name as I loped through a
softball game once said, "Them sneakers have never
moved so slow." Still, they are my present from a superb
major leaguer, and so a kind of totem. I didn't want them
dirtied with black ash.

"We'll get messed up," I said. "We can try again next
weekend."

"We don't have visitation next weekend. Come on. Just
pitch a few."

Clumps of forsythia bloomed yellow on a knoll and
arching willows showed a promise of green. But the April
wind cut sharply through our jackets. This spring day was
better admired from indoors.

1

The boy's large eyes fixed me with a demanding look. "Just pitch a few," he said. Then, seductively, "After that, I'll pitch and *you* can hit."

His name is Roger and he has a sturdy twelve-year-old body and a passionate excitement at being alive. "I'm studying The Renaissance," he announced recently, as I was preparing papers for a tax audit.

"Good," I said. "The Renaissance," I said. "Who the hell was Michelangelo?"

"Wait," Roger cried. "Don't give me the answer. I know. Michelangelo put statues in the gardens of the Medici."

He is constantly delighting me in unexpected ways, but ours is a spiky relationship. His mother and I had good times, very good times, and when the bad times came they were as bad as any I have known. Then Roger found himself between two parents whom he loved and five lawyers whom he did not know, all clawing toward a divorce settlement he would not understand. Roger has not pieced things together yet. Sometimes he rages. Sometimes he grows morose. But we can talk about The Renaissance. And we play ball.

He carried a new aluminum bat as he ran toward a sooty home plate. Like major leaguers, children run to the plate for batting practice.

He hits lefthanded. We started working toward that nine years ago when we all lived together, and now as he took an open stance, he chattered directions. "Don't throw too hard. I haven't started working out yet. Don't throw me curves. Let me get my swing grooved. Okay. Come on."

I began to throw high pitches at medium speed. My older son stationed himself in right center, generous enough to shag for his brother, unhappy as I with the April wind.

Roger lunged. Four years with the Little League in Ridgefield, Connecticut. Four seasons under coaches who work for IBM, or sell insurance or pilot 727s, and nobody has taught him, or been able to teach him, that a good hitter does not lunge.

"Keep your head still," I said.

The boy's mouth tightened. He had not come to learn. He wanted to show me how far he could hit my pitching, swinging his own metal bat in his own way.

Very well, young man, I thought. Today in the April cold, you'll get a playing lesson. Subject: He who lunges never hits .300.

I threw hard with an easy motion. Roger swung late. I threw easily with a big motion. He swung early. I tried to jam him, but the ball drifted inside toward his knees. Roger made a graceful arcing leap. The ball skidded into the backstop. He lay face down, shaking on the earth.

I hurried to him. "Sorry. Sorry. You all right?"

He rolled over, blackening his jacket. He was shaking with defiant young laughter. "You couldn't hurt me," he said.

We grinned and at once the playing lesson was done. He had earned the right to pitches he could hit. Roger began scattering line drives. His brother, the outfielder, retired. Roger looped a fly to center. There was no one to retrieve the ball but me. He bounced sharply through the middle. Another job for an aging chilly righthander. He lashed a high inside pitch clear to a ditch at the border of right field.

"Now we'll just play pepper," I said, when I returned with the ball.

He insisted on borrowing my bat. Thirty-two ounces. A fat-barreled Ron Santo model. Either Roger did not know the rules of pepper or he didn't know how suddenly strong he had become. I made a pepper toss. Roger whipped the big bat. We stood thirty feet apart. The blackened baseball hurtled at my nose. I threw a glove up and deflected the ball and stumbled. Sitting on charred grass, I remembered a transcendent reality of baseball. The ball is hard. It is something to fear. Forty years ago I learned that from my father in Brooklyn fields that have vanished under high-rises. Seventy years ago, he learned that from his father on fields that have disappeared under slum. And now my son, in careless, innocent excitement, had reinforced a family lesson old as the century.

Roger came toward me slowly. The Ron Santo model seemed almost as big as he. His face was white. "Dad, I didn't mean to hit a liner at your face."

Getting up, glad still to have a nose, I fell back on a Wayne-Bogart gambit. "Gosh, kid, I didn't know you cared."

"Sure I care," Roger said and he put an arm around my waist. We started hiking to a distant house where splits of maple crackled in a fireplace. There we could sit before the fire and talk baseball.

What would I tell him? Of Stan Musial, most gentle of athletes, whose swing was like a viper's lash? Or of the day when Early Wynn brushed Mickey Mantle, who bounced up and hit a single? Wynn was so furious that before he threw another pitch, he went into a careful pick-off move. Then he hit Mantle with his throw, knocking him to the ground beside first base. "That son of a bitch is so mean," Mantle complained, "he'd fucking knock you down in the dugout." Or about Victor Pellot Power, of Arecibo, Puerto Rico, whom the Yankees traded in 1954 for announced reasons that are not worth remembering? The real reasons were that Power was black and Latin and reputedly liked the company of white women. Victor Pellot Power, a solid .290 hitter, seven times won the Gold Glove awarded to the best first baseman in the American League, but he won it for clubs without the moralistic, some would say prejudiced, front office of the old Yankees. (When I saw Power in the Puerto Rican hill town of Caguas years later, he demonstrated that the Yankees had been correct in at least one thought. Power liked white women well enough to have married a compact, smoldering blonde whose name is Ada.)

The game begins with sons and fathers, fathers and sons. The theme is older than the English novel, older than *Hamlet,* old at least as the Torah. You play baseball with love and you play baseball to win and you play baseball with terror, but always against that backdrop, fathers and sons. Stan Musial describes his father, Lukasc, as a wiry Polish immigrant, who spoke broken English and didn't understand a stolen base. His son wanted only to play ball.

After high school a scout from the University of Pittsburgh offered Stan a basketball scholarship and the family was torn with civil strife. "A free college education," Lukasc told his son, "that is the best thing. You will go to college, Stash."

"I don't want to go to college, Pop. I want to be a ball player."

The argument warmed until Mary Musial won the day for her son. "This is a free country," she told Lukasc. "The boy is free not to go to college."

Stan Musial in Ebbets Field was the best hitter I ever saw and he insists, as few men do, that he never once felt fear of a baseball. "I saw it good," he says. "It didn't scare me." Although Musial is a man of regal pride, braggadocio does not touch him. You do best to take him at his word. But then he adds, "Of course I was in the majors four or five years before I got to be a real confident hitter."

Not only the baseball kindles fright. There is the horror of naked failure, striking out, sinking into a slump, falling into the minors, dropping out of baseball, coming home to a stern European father who shakes his head. Young Stan Musial did not want to drop out of baseball. He had seen his father's working life too vividly. Lukasc Musial labored in a steel mill in a dreary river town called Donora, Pennsylvania, where a hellish smog once strangled sixty persons. For Stan Musial, vying against a father he loved, baseball was freedom road.

My own father, who taught and edited and never lost his passionate excitement at being alive, hit a baseball hard. Two months before his heart stopped he was lining high drives to center on Monhegan Island, off the coast of

Maine. By then he was fifty-two and I was twenty-five, but I could not hit a ball as far as he. Good speed. Quick bat. No power. He had hoped I would grow taller and stand someday beside Jake Daubert and Zack Wheat, the heroes of his own sandlot days. Then he was dead and people who admired his eidetic memory and his own understanding of The Renaissance told me how fine it must have been to grow up at his side and to talk seriously with him about serious things, such as the gardens of the Medici. I don't believe we ever did. We talked seriously (and joyously) about baseball. That was a serious thing and that was enough.

You learn to leave some mysteries alone. At twenty-eight, I was susceptible to suggestions that I explain—not describe but explain—baseball in America. I published in small quarterlies. I addressed a Columbia seminar. I developed a showy proficiency at responding to editors who asked me to "equate the game in terms of Americana."

Such phrases now bang against my brain like toothaches. I never look at the old pieces any more, but I remember some generalizations I drew.

Baseball is not played against a clock. (But neither is tennis, golf or four-handed gin rummy.)

Baseball rules have barely changed across generations. (Neither have the rules of water polo.)

The ball field itself is a mystic creation, the Stonehenge of America. That is, the bases are a magic ninety feet apart. Think how often a batter is thrown out by half a step, compared to instances when he outruns a hit to shortstop. But artificial surfaces have lately changed the nature, if not the dimensions, of the diamond. A ground ball at Riverfront Stadium is more a missile than the same grounder bouncing on the honest grass of Wrigley Field. Yet at last look, baseball in Cincinnati seemed to be surviving.

Suppose the bases were set eighty or eighty-six feet apart. The fielders would simply position themselves differently and a ground ball to short would still be a ground ball to short, six to three in everybody's scorebook.

I do believe this: that baseball's inherent rhythm, minutes and minutes of passivity erupting into seconds of frenzied action, matches an attribute of the American character. But no existential proclamation, nor any tortured neo-Freudianism, nor any outburst of popular sociology, not even, or least of all, my own, explains baseball's lovelock on the American heart.

You learn to let some mysteries alone, and when you do, you find they sing themselves.

I had been lunching in a Manhattan tower with a command post of editors from *Sports Illustrated* magazine. B. Peter Carry, youngest of their senior staff, is intense and driving and skilled and second baseman on the magazine's slow-pitch softball team.

Bob Ottum, the articles editor, is droll, wiry and rich in counterpunching humor. Roy Terrell is the managing editor. When Terrell was hired in 1955, someone described him as "crew-cut, from Texas, an ex-Marine and despite all that a nice guy."

"We'd like you to take a look at baseball in America,"

Pete Carry said. "In fact we'd like to give your piece that title, 'Baseball in America.' "

That's a label, not a title, I was thinking as drinks arrived. I put off further thought.

"Sort of see how the game is doing," Ottum said.

"Attendance," Carry said. "The health of major league franchises. The character of players. Is there a new breed? What's the link between the Little Leagues and the majors? Can the game survive the people who run it? We ought to get a helluva piece."

We settled on a set of three articles and I began planning a baseball odyssey, work that goes easily when one is in good company, well fed and stationary. I'd want to consider a winning major league baseball team, plump with prosperity, and match that franchise against a losing ball club, straining to cover its paychecks. Go ride the buses of the minors and live with young men who win and lose in solitude. Find children at play, but not Little League children. The joys and griefs of Little League life have been examined in greater detail than Nixon's final days. Discover children not necessarily supervised, uniformed or washed. The people. Seek out an antiorganization man and see how baseball deals with what its ruling class calls "bolsheviks." Bolsheviks, indeed. Had the 1976 presidential voting been limited to the men who own major league franchises, William McKinley would have outpolled Mr. Carter.

Look for someone born out of time, who spent his skills in the old Negro leagues, quite literally black obscurity. Contrast him with a white, who ran a baseball career into a fortune. Consider a star today in the fullness of his youth and sinew. Johnny Bench. But it was April. Who knew what kind of season Bench would have?

"You'll probably have to travel the whole country," Carry said.

I would want to travel the whole country. Baseball in a New England factory town, where the ball field sits on a river bank and the stands are wooden slats, is at once history. Baseball at the Astrodome in Houston, where the scoreboard flashes electronic pictures, the temperature is perennially 72 degrees and lucite panels forming the roof put off the sky and even any sense of place, suggests the future.

I could find ball players from the old racist South and ball players from the factory towns, but where to see free-running children who wanted to be ball players? When we were young and ran free, we all wanted to be ball players. I have walked ghetto streets in Cleveland and the South Bronx and Detroit, and baseball now is blank of meaning there. That is a crippling truth about the heroin highs and wine drunks of a ghetto boyhood. The young grow up not knowing how to dream.

I'd have a lot to think about, but it had been an extraordinary magazine lunch, Terrell said.

At home, the workroom is small and cluttered and bare, a chair, a desk, a cigarette-scarred table, a glaring lighting fixture, set within azure walls. An interviewer has described the room as spartan. Sometimes when sentences behave, the workroom is my favorite place on earth. But

most of the time sentences do not behave and the workroom is a concentration camp. Since ' am given to hyper-
bole, I call it Auschwitz.

Alone after the lunch, I set to thinking. What the magazine editors and I had been discussing was not really a set
of magazine stories at all. If I could find the right cast, and
seek out the most compelling places, I'd need more space
than *Sports Illustrated* could offer. I'd need the length
and freedom of a book. A little frightened now, I poured
a Scotch.

The baseball bolshevik came easily. Early Wynn. We
had run together and flown together and greeted several
dawns. Now after an outspoken lifetime in baseball, Wynn
was on the outside, selling boats. The rich man would be
Stanley Frank Musial, the millhand's son from Pennsylvania, who owns restaurants and hotels in several states.

Monte Irvin of the Baseball Commissioner's office suggested Artie Wilson, a black shortstop of great skills and
greater anonymity, who was selling cars on a lot outside
Portland, Oregon.

The minor league team would best be in New England,
where children played varieties of baseball in 1800. Houston was the troubled franchise. The Astros had their
Dome, but they had traded away a better team than they
were fielding. Now no one came to see them play, and
credit companies ruled the franchise. The Dodgers offered the richest vein. Years of contending clubs and
years of phenomenal attendance had made a fortune for
their ruling family, the O'Malleys out of County Mayo,
Ireland.

Lawrence Ritter, the author of *The Glory of Their Times,* suggested where to find free-running children. "In Puerto Rico," Ritter said, "every town has its team and everybody who can play does play, kids, amateurs, semi-pros, professional. It's like the continental United States in the 1930s."

Buz Wyeth of Harper & Row suggested that I visit Bill Veeck, the irreverent promoter, who was running the Chicago White Sox again, after fourteen years in the limbo of lecture circuits. Once Veeck had said, "My time is past, the way P. T. Barnum's time is past. I'm an individualist. Baseball has become a syndicate business." But Veeck *was* back. How would this great, gregarious loner fare among the tax lawyers and conglomerate men who dominate baseball ownership today?

At length I needed a college team. As I remembered college baseball in the Northeast, the game was dreary. Usually the weather was bad and after watching, say, Pee Wee Reese, it was hard to glory in an Ivy League short-stop. But in some gentler climates, I had heard, the college game was exciting and sometimes remarkably well played.

A year before, I had attended a dinner at Shea Stadium with, among others, Wally Moon, a fine outfielder who played for the Dodgers and the Cardinals. Together we had seen senility embrace Charles Dillon Stengel. In form, with all cerebral arteries functioning, Stengel was a man of wit, subtlety and shrewdness. His incoherence, about which so much has been written, was the most coherent incoherence of his era.

Once we were watching Sam Snead take a turn at batting practice. Snead missed a half-dozen low-breaking pitches. "Throw it up around his eyes," a Yankee yelled. The pitcher did and Snead clubbed a long drive to left center field.

"Imagine that," Stengel said. "A golfer who's a high-ball hitter."

A magazine, *Sports Illustrated* as a matter of fact, offered me a job in 1954, contingent on my composing a good story about the power pitcher Allie Reynolds. Stengel distrusted magazines, but since I had covered the Yankees briefly for the New York *Herald Tribune* the old man grouped me in that school of journalism he called "my writers."

"This important to ya, kid?" he said.

"Yes."

He took a drink and inhaled. "Reynolds," he said, "is the greatest I have seen, which is both ways, starting and relieving, and I seen the great ones, Mathewson and I seen Cy Young, and I wondered who that fat old guy was, which shows what a dumb young punk I was. You could look it up."

After Milwaukee defeated the Yankees, four games to three, in the 1957 World Series, a television reporter asked Stengel if he thought his team had "choked, collapsed under the pressure out there."

"Do you choke on your fucking microphone?" Stengel said. He quickly whirled and began rubbing his buttocks.

"Ya see," he told me later, "I said 'fuck' to ruin his audio. Then when I started scratching my ass I was ruining his video. He ain't gonna ask me a question like that again."

During the dinner at Shea, Stengel's rambling talk lacked wit, shrewdness, even sense. He was an eighty-five-year-old man, muttering disconnected fragments to himself. Wally Moon sat across from me, and after averting eyes for a time, we exchanged looks, wondering, I suppose, how long this would go on and how on earth anyone could get Stengel to sit down.

The organist began "The Band Played On." Stengel continued talking through his private fog. The organist played louder. Someone began to sing.

> Oh, Casey would waltz with a strawberry blonde,
> And the band played on.

Stengel's lips still moved, but you could not hear him any more.

> He'd light up the floor with the girl he adored,
> And the band played on.

At last old Casey Stengel recognized the din around him. Grimacing, he collapsed into a chair, then tried to smile.

"Terrible," Wally Moon said.

"Particularly if you knew the way he was," I said.

We sat in silence.

"But the game keeps on," Moon said. "The game. I coach at a little college in Arkansas. You ought to see some of the young people I have. Pretty town called Siloam Springs. If you ever have a chance to come out, we'd love to have you and maybe you'd like to meet the kids.

So there was my college team. John Brown University. I'd have to pack some bags and find my way to Siloam Springs, Arkansas.

The weather was warming. This could be the most exciting baseball season I had known.

1

The Town Where Someone Drives a Kaiser Car

Alongside the two-lane blacktop across northeast Oklahoma, the land rolls bare and poor. Outside of villages called Broken Arrow and Chouteau lie shacks and rusty trailers where survivors of the Cherokee Nation live clumped in poverty. This is not farming country. It is hard, red intractable soil that we have left to the Indians.

Then abruptly, as the highway crosses into Arkansas and into the cultivated village of Siloam Springs, a wonder of pastureland appears. Siloam Springs is Wally Moon's domain. Wallace Wade Moon, late of the St. Louis Cardinals and the Los Angeles Dodgers. Now head baseball coach at John Brown University. Student body: 600. Team batting average: .371.

On the telephone Moon said he had a few minutes of

desk work, and waiting for him I asked the lady behind the front desk of the East Gate Motel to explain the relative prosperity of Benton County, Arkansas.

"It's a little embarrassing," she said. Behind spectacles, her eyes were pale and pleasant.

"How so?"

"Chicken droppings," the lady said. "I guess that's the best way to put it." Then she explained. Northwest Arkansas had been poor as Oklahoma until after World War II, when some men decided to try chicken farming in the Ozark foothills. "That went pretty good, you might say," the lady continued, "but it sure left a lot of chicken droppings. They smelled. So the farmers spread the stuff across the fields and hills and after a few years the soil got a darn sight richer. Real good grass grew. After that some other people brought in cattle and the cattle grazed good and times got better. Not that we don't have some poor, but Benton County's doing fine right now.

"Truth is, though"—the lady's eyes darted to make sure we were alone—"the economy here is built on chicken shit."

"Yes, ma'am," I said.

Wally Moon had talked rather less of chickens and more of a high sky and gentle streams when we shared dinner after Casey Stengel's sad speech the year before. Wally Moon, outfielder and batsman, played twelve major league years across the 1950s and '60s. He wore his hair short and his thick black eyebrows met and he had the look of a Confederate cavalry captain. But he was a decent, tolerant man, with a master's degree from Texas

A&M, wholly dedicated to squeezing the last base hit out of each turn at bat in every season.

The St. Louis Cardinals called him up in 1954, just as they sold Enos Slaughter, a portly, combative legend, to the Yankees. On the Sunday before Moon broke in, the St. Louis *Post-Dispatch* published a front-page picture of Enos Slaughter, weeping with grief into a large white handkerchief.

Moon came from Arkansas delta country, and the first time he saw a major league game, he was playing in it. The St. Louis crowd if not hostile was at least belligerently neutral. They loved the legend Moon had been hired to replace. In his first time at bat in his first major league game Moon pulled a home run over the right-field pavilion of the old Busch Stadium and into Grand Boulevard beyond. That year Enos Slaughter batted .248 for the New York Yankees. Moon hit .304 and became rookie of the year.

Five seasons later with the Los Angeles Dodgers, he perfected his opposite-field hitting. The Dodgers played in the Coliseum then and left-field screen, the players said, was only a medium pee away from home. Moon hit nineteen home runs, mostly to left, led the league in triples, hit twenty-six doubles, and a Dodger team of shreds and patches established itself in Los Angeles by winning the World Series from the White Sox.

When Moon's skills eroded, he and his wife, Bettye, debated city and country life. They had five children and he could earn more money in an urban center. But Wally remembered good days with his father, Bert, hunting and hiking through the woods of Benton County. Now there was an offer to try Benton County again, as head coach at John Brown, a small Christian Evangelical school.

"It's worked out," Wally had said, at the dinner in Shea Stadium. "I think I'll have a real fine team next year."

Old ball players chattered loudly about the room. "Isn't the pace in Siloam Springs a little hectic?" I said.

"Yeah," Moon said, grinning, "but I've got a retreat in the Carolina mountains. When the rat race gets too bad, I head up there."

The Moons live in a rambling ranch set on two hundred acres, four miles east of Siloam, a town with an artists' colony, no daily newspaper, light industry and springs that were once said to have possessed medicinal properties. At the Chamber of Commerce on University Street, you can purchase Volume One of *Hico: A Heritage—Siloam Springs History* by Maggie Aldridge Smith. Volume One runs 445 pages and costs $10.50.

Arkansas differs from Missouri, because it did not lie along the classic pathways west. Untraveled, it developed more slowly than other states, which troubles certain natives but delights tourists. Large sections of Arkansas are free of interstate highways, Holiday Inns, Pizza Huts. All one finds are soft hills, thick with pine and pin oak, clear streams and bright upland meadows. Siloam Springs, in the northwest corner of the state, lies off by itself, where many waters meet, under a wider, clearer sky than one finds in the East or California.

Close by Siloam, stone houses are clustered in a community of Italian-Americans called Tontitown. There sunny hillsides glow with grape arbors. The Moons, worldly people, are not admirers of Arkansas *vin ordinaire*. There is even a story of someone dining in Tontitown and asking the waiter what vintage wine was available.

"Thursday," the waiter said.

The man looked disappointed. "I would have prefered Tuesday," he said.

Siloam Springs itself is dry. According to Maggie Smith's history, early settlers in Hico profited by selling whiskey to Cherokees in the Oklahoma Territory. The town changed its name from Hico to Siloam, and having prospered in the liquor business, found the paths of righteousness and closed the bars.

The strongest single tradition is religion. Within Oak Hill Cemetery you find buried near one another J. B. Lineback, of the Confederate Army, and Abell Pickering, who fought for the Union. Houses on knolls and meadows bespeak the town's variety. They range from Victorian gingerbread to contemporary ranch. But the strong tradition—variations on a liturgical theme—shows in the disparity of churches.

Pastor Roy Hilton of Siloam Springs Christian Center wears an Ahab beard and says, "Jesus is the bridge over troubled water." He has driven a taxi to raise money for the Christian Center, which he describes as a "twenty-four-hour refuge for the oppressed, the stranded, the homeless." Roy Hilton could be comfortable in a storefront church in Harlem. The Bethel United Methodist Church, under Dr. A. P. Vohs, offers Sunday school, Bible class and conventional Middle American religiosity. The

Christ Temple Church of Pentecostal Assembly of the World convened for a time under trees. According to the Reverend Luke L. Church, of Christ Temple, "Recently the church has seen two people raised up from the dead, goiters removed, those that had been crippled healed, demons cast out and many converted."

John Brown University, where Moon coaches baseball and runs the athletic program, was founded in 1919 by John Elward Brown, a Salvation Army lieutenant, whose motto was "To search, to seek, to find and not to yield." His son, Dr. John Brown, Jr., presides. Although the university now draws its six hundred students from forty states, it remains doggedly rural and religious. Room and board cost $2,400 annually, roughly a third of room and board at Princeton. One can study Shakespearean drama at John Brown and also major in building construction. The Music Department offers a bachelor of arts degree with a major in "music for the business person." Each spring semester brings a pause for a Bible Missionary Conference.

John Brown, the president of the university that bears his father's name and his own, is an impassioned ball fan. He admires Wally Moon and he has had the patience to give Moon a decade to achieve competitive baseball. Without recruiting, scouting or limitless scholarship programs, Moon has made a small Bible college into a baseball power across ten years. He knows he has done it. He is proud. "And Dr. Brown shares my pride," he says, "although we don't share the same ideas about my salary."

Moon smiles easily. He respects money in a mature, low-keyed way.

A giant red oak towers over the Moons' home, sixty feet off a back road. Inside one finds a cheerful babble of children. Wally Joe, husky and twenty-three, talked of his free-form poetry and his work toward a master's degree at the University of Arkansas. He wears eyeglasses. He had wanted to play major league ball. He suffered from poor depth perception. Four daughters, from twelve to twenty, were bright, mannerly, attractive. Their interests swept from baton-twirling to Clementi sonatas. Moon said grace and we dined on Arkansas grass-fed beef.

Then, in the old-fashioned way, the ladies went about their chores, while Moon and I retired to a sunroom, crowded with pictures and trophies. On one wall he glowers fiercely from an old *Sports Illustrated* cover, beside a caption announcing: "The Spirit of the Gashouse Gang."

"Actually," Moon said, "the spunkiest team of all was those 1959 Dodgers. Not the best. Some of the old Brooklyn Dodgers on the way down. Fellows like Koufax and Drysdale on the way up. But I never played on a club that wanted to win more." He'd admired Walt Alston, Moon said, and he'd roomed with Koufax and told Sandy that for all his stuff, he was tipping his pitches. But those were old times and Wally had a new story to tell.

Across four days in May, the John Brown baseball team hurled itself into the Arkansas division of a tournament sponsored by the National Association for Intercollegiate Athletics. Traditionally, this is a small-college tournament and it is true that Southern California is not eligible. But NAIA teams include universities with student bodies of ten thousand. Dr. Brown's Christian Evangelicals, Moon conceded, would not be favored to win the national championship. But he wanted very much to win District 17. "And we can," he said. "On form, we can."

A small caravan had set forth east toward Pine Bluff, Arkansas, at 5:10 on the evening of May 5. Moon's lead station wagon pulled an equipment trailer, on which a broken tail light winked and winked. "It looked like he was turning right the whole trip," said Chuck Gardner, the shortstop. The first opponent would be the University of Arkansas at Pine Bluff, a squad of fifteen blacks and three whites. Jerome Maxie, the only black on the John Brown varsity, said he had a cousin attending Pine Bluff. "One cousin," Gardner said, "and a lot of brothers."

After a restless, rainy day at the Admiral Benbow Inn, the Golden Eagles chattered through batting practice Friday at a tidy little ball park called Bush Field. A cyclone fence in right rose only 280 feet away. Beyond it lay a narrow street and a white house, fronted by a yard. Moon's squad has power. The boys could clear both fence and street, and now a curious comedy began. On his budget, Moon needs every baseball he has. On a budget of their own, the couple in the white house intended to protect hearth, home, mortgage and windows.

When one of Moon's players slammed a long drive to the yard, a heavy lady burst through the door and took the drive on two bounces. Then she hurried back into the house with the baseball. She slammed the door.

Moon assigned Joe Huss, a lefthanded pitcher, to stand in front of the yard. The door opened. "Git away from here afore we git the shotgun," the lady called. There may be more Confederate captain to Wally Moon than I know.

Huss stood his ground. He retrieved four straight batting-practice homers. No shotgun appeared, but the woman's husband did. Two-on-one, but Huss had youth and conditioning going for him. Still, the woman finally beat him to a baseball.

At home plate Gardner, a handsome, brown-eyed Texan, whose batting average was then .443, shook his head. "I used to have neighbors like that," he said. "Their only purpose in life was to run someone out of the yard."

The players plotted revenge. A phantom pitch. A phantom swing. A dozen voices shouted, "There it goes." Huss leaped high, as though trying to make a catch. The door opened again. The heavy woman rushed out. She shook her head and muttered. There was no baseball, because no baseball had been hit. The John Brown players laughed the laugh of Eagles.

They did not laugh the next day. A Pine Bluff right-hander called Carl Nicholson overpowered them and won, 3 to 0. Now they would have to beat a tougher team, Arkansas Tech, and then win three out of four in order to finish first in District 17. "If we can't win four in a row, we won't be going anyplace anyway," Moon said in the clubhouse before the game. His team awoke, won 13 to 2, and started kidding Dave Stockstill, a freshman outfielder, who was batting .425. "Is it true," someone wanted to know, "that you carry a portable calculator, so you can figure your batting average before you go to sleep?" College humor is gentler than what one hears in the major leagues. The players are learning the game and they are learning how to needle.

Most are on scholarship. They address Moon as "Coach," often in the deferential way a man in pain says "Doctor." Coach Moon imposes rules. No bean balls. Bench jockeying is permitted, but within limits that would make Jim Bouton blanch. Moon is a devout Methodist and none of his players "may blaspheme the name of the Lord." As I suppose Bouton would point out, this makes it permissible to tell an umpire to fuck off, but not to say "God damn bad call."

That night John Brown split a double-header. They would have to win both ball games on Sunday or be eliminated.

Moon's team won the first game against the Pine Bluffs, 13 to 4. In the second game, Maxie slammed a home run. The only John Brown U. black raised a clenched fist over his head as he touched home plate. John Brown hit every pitcher the Pine Bluffs could present. When the final out came at 8:05, the score was John Brown 24, Pine Bluff 8.

"We'll eat at a steak house I know," Wally Moon promised. The steak house was closed. Pine Bluff, Arkansas, was buttoning down for a Sunday night. "There's another place," he said and at the Riverfront Inn, an open restaurant beckoned like a sunburst. Eighteen players, a staff of three and a newspaperman sat down. One waitress was available to serve them. Dick Stockton, the newspaperman, took notes. Dave Stockstill devoured eighteen rolls before his meal arrived.

Between Pine Bluff and Fort Smith, a downpour struck. The caravan climbed into the Ozark Mountains and fog. Moon held the lead car to ten miles an hour. The players, still in uniforms, slept sitting up, and Moon, still in uniform, drove on. "Boys," he said, as they stumbled from the cars into a wet Siloam Springs dawn, "baseball is a game of endurance."

"As a coach," I said the next night amid Moon's trophies, "I guess your strongest point is cautious driving."

"As a coach," Moon said, "my strongest point is batting. I teach them to hold their heads still and keep the bat back. Strike zone? They're not ready for that yet, and I don't believe in teaching too many things at once. Just develop a quick compact swing. If I have a weak point, or a point where I lack confidence, that would be pitching." He looked across a darkening field. "You're still learning baseball, aren't you? I'm still learning and I'm forty-six. Man, this is a difficult sport to learn."

The next afternoon John Brown played a twilight game against the University of Tulsa, which has a student body of nine thousand. The Siloam Springs ball park has been leveled in a glade, and as game time approached and the Franklin Electric plant and the Ace Plastics factory closed, pick-up trucks and motorbikes and Chevrolets and Fords filled the lot behind center field. There is no admission charge to watch the Eagles. Minor league ball is gone forever from Siloam Springs. John Brown University is the town team.

The fans sat in wooden bleachers and on grassy banks. "A kind of Greek theater," Bettye Moon announced. Two major league scouts mixed with the crowd. Both Fred Hawn of the Cardinals and Milt Bolling of the Boston Red

Sox had come. Chuck Gardner, the shortstop, was their primary quarry.

The Eagles warmed up smartly with fine infield play. The outfielders showed strong young arms. Moon started Ron Rhodes, a junior righthander who had won eight straight games, and the team jumped ahead when Gardner doubled home one run in the first inning and two more in the second. But Tulsa came back when Bruce Humphrey slammed a 380-foot home run over the cyclone fence in center field, and Tulsa kept coming.

These teams were good. Unlike college squads in the Northern tier, they had started working out of doors in February. Each club had already played forty games. But they are collegians and collegians make mistakes. By the last inning Tulsa had drawn ahead, 6 to 5. Gardner led off with a single, a murderous drive that hurtled past the pitcher's left ear. A sacrifice moved him to second. He was the tying run. Randy Rouse grounded to shortstop and Gardner tried to go to third.

That never works. The rule is as old as baseball. A runner cannot advance from second to third on a ball hit to the left side of the infield. Gardner was out by ten feet, and when Dave Stockstill blinked at a fast ball, knee-high on the outside corner of the plate, the Golden Eagles had been beaten.

Moon's lips were pressed together. He does not like to lose. "You can never advance on that play, Wally," I said.

He shook his head and spat, then looked less fierce. "But the kid wanted to score so damn bad."

Lightning interrupted the next day's workout. In downtown Siloam Springs a siren sounded one steady harsh note. "That's a tornado alert," Moon said, "but don't worry till it warbles. A warbling siren means a funnel's been sighted." We repaired to the Quonset hut that is Moon's clubhouse and he began to tell his players about yesterday's game.

He had spoken privately with Gardner and now he had more general things to say. "My analysis," he began, "is that we got beat because Tulsa wanted to win more than we did. It wasn't a tournament game for us. We had a hard trip the other day. But that doesn't matter. However you feel, when you walk through that gate and onto the field, you've got to kick yourself in the butt. Here or in the majors. I can tell you from personal experience that across a major league season, your butt ends up pretty sore. But you've got to do it.

"Now, Ron," he said to Rhodes, "you remember when first base was open and I went out to the mound and I told you to pitch around the hitter."

Rhodes nodded gravely.

"In the majors I would have said deliberately walk him. That was the play. But we're here to learn and I want you to learn what I mean by pitching around a hitter.

"In that situation, with a runner in scoring position the hitter is eager. Start him with a fast ball all the way in on his belly. He's so eager he may swing, but he's not going to hurt you off a pitch like that. Then when you curve him, get it in the dirt. Not just low. In the dirt. He's still eager. If he walks, you aren't hurt, and if he swings at a bouncing curve, you aren't hurt, either. But you gave him a pitch he could hit and he hit it and it scored a run, and that's what we lost by. One run.

"For you hitters, look at that situation in reverse. Control your eagerness. That's a mental discipline. There's a lot of mental discipline in the game. But you've got nothing to be ashamed of, any of you. Tulsa is a good club. They wanted the game more than you did and they got it."

Rain beat fiercely on the iron roof. "Do you have any questions?" Moon asked me.

"I'd like to ask how many of you gentlemen hope to play in the major leagues." The boys, eighteen to twenty-one, from towns like Texarkana, Paducah and Hurley, Missouri, looked at one another, embarrassed. Then slowly, shyly, in the Quonset hut under a downpour, all eighteen of Wally Moon's Golden Eagles raised their hands. To the man, they played Little League ball and enjoyed it. To the man, they ached to play in the major leagues. "I'm not looking for a bonus," one of Moon's best players said. "If I had the money, I'd pay *them* to sign me."

"How many have a chance?" I asked Moon after the players left.

"Probably none," Moon said. "The shortstop is good, but he's twenty-one years old. I've seen another college shortstop just about as good and he's eighteen. A big three years. Then you figure beyond all the college shortstops, there are all the boys already in the minors, playing 140 games a year, kids from all over the country and Latin America, and you realize what the odds are against Chuck

Gardner. He'll play minor league ball. So will a few of the others. But most of them will go on from here to teach and coach. I want them to enjoy the game, but I want them to learn technique and conduct and discipline as well." Moon stood up. "Maybe they can pass on what I can give them to others."

We went to a Rotary meeting then. We stood to pledge allegiance and we sang "America the Beautiful" under the fervid conducting of a local doctor named John Moose. I remembered morning chapels in my own grade school then and how we had to sing:

> Cast thy burden upon the Lord
> And he will sustain . . .

Two, three, four, beat the pudgy right hand of Miss Mac . . .

> . . . thee.

"Now," Miss Mac told me once, before the entire fourth-grade class, "it is not absolutely necessary for you to sing. It might be better if you only moved your lips."

Oh, I would find a vengeance for Miss Mac. I taught myself to play "Cast Thy Burden" on a harmonica and refused to go to concerts for fifteen years, thus missing Toscanini, Koussevitzky and the prime of Jascha Heifetz.

But nobody ever told me not to swing a bat and so my boldest and most secret dream was to be able to hit as well as Wally Moon would hit years later.

> America! America!
> God shed his grace on thee.

In Siloam, where many streams converge, at last I evened matters with Miss Mac. Standing beside Wally Moon, I sang "America the Beautiful," not only moved my lips but sang, though not as well as he.

For all the fresh clean-shaven faces of Coach Moon's Golden Eagles, the trip to Siloam Springs was a voyage into the past. Leaving town, I saw a sign that read:

GUITAR LESSONS

PIANO TUNING

GOSPEL PIANO

Then I passed someone driving a yellow Kaiser car. I believe they stopped making Kaisers in 1955.

2

The Franchise Business

1

After the brilliant pellucid sky that sheltered Siloam Springs, the yellow air of Los Angeles looked as oppressive as a shroud. I would not propose a flight west into Los Angeles as an advertisement for America. Meadows grow into spiny mountains, which flatten to desert. Finally, under an urban pall, the city appears.

Most of Wally Moon's Golden Eagles see Siloam Springs as a pretty place. Yet most would give such things as they possess to drive to Tulsa and then fly into the smog of Southern California.

Professionally, their judgment is correct. They are ball players. Across the two decades since the Dodgers left Brooklyn, a new team, and indeed a new style, have been born at Los Angeles. Sandy Koufax would not agree. Andy

Messersmith did not agree. Johnny Bench might or might not argue. But for most athletes, Los Angeles is the place to play ball.

Dodger Stadium is a triumph of baseball design. The grass is real. The shape proclaims baseball. Dodger Stadium is not a multipurpose arena. It is a ball park. The Dodgers train in luxury at Vero Beach, Florida, and then repair by the team's private Boeing 720 to a California season in the sun. Then they are coached, urged, paid, cajoled, demanded, begged to finish ahead of the Cincinnati Reds.

As a business, the Dodgers need to draw 2,100,000 admissions per season to break even. Running a team that grandly is a naked arrogance in baseball. Many owners have to attract only one million fans. But night after night the Dodgers draw their big crowds. Year after year the ledgers smile in black. If one had limitless capital, perfect investment advice and, implausibly, caught the Dodger management evaluating its franchise at a figure lower than the national debt, the Los Angeles Dodgers would be the best of teams to buy.

Driving east from Beverly Hills down Sunset Boulevard one sees decline. The mansions fade. The Strip appears. Clubs like The Body Shop advertise naked dancers. The street narrows. Laundromats alternate with small, sad bars. Mercedeses no longer clog the lanes. Then following a too-small sign, one turns left, toward 1000 Elysian Park Avenue. Elysium. The fields of praise. You drive past batteries of toll-takers, closed because it is twelve hours before game time, and the Dodger parking lots appear, multileveled parking so that, in the California manner, you expend minimal leather and effort to reach your seat. Traffic lights direct you in the lot. The private lot of the Los Angeles Dodgers has its own traffic lights, even as Times Square.

When you park at the so-called "office level," you notice that, unlike Times Square, the lot is clean. Wandering the Schlossgarten in Stuttgart once I noticed similar cleanliness. "Of course," my companion said. "In Germany the penalty for littering is execution." In Los Angeles the Dodgers have to hire platoons of sanitation men to work this Württemberg-Baden effect. It is a matter of both style and extravagance that they do.

Troughs of flowers near the entrance suggest gaiety. A *Baseballfest*. Do people go to Dodger Stadium to behold flowers? Not primarily, but people have stayed away from other ball parks because of ambient filth.

The man who owns the Dodgers did not like *The Boys of Summer*, a book I wrote celebrating baseball, life, the courage to be new and certain men who spent a decade winning pennants for the Dodgers. A Los Angeles morning had broken summery and dense, light smog hovering under a mustard sky, after a night when the Dodgers defeated the Cincinnati Reds, 5 to 0. Walter Francis O'Malley, a compelling seventy-three-year-old paterfamilias who mixes Quaker parsimony, pagan ferocity and Irish-Catholic charm, looked up darkly from sheaves of correspondence. He did not say, "Hello." He did not say, "How are you?" Instead, he growled in a Tammany bass, "This time are you going to write something positive?"

At such moments, I long to utter an infinite retort, at once deflating the critic and placing my published work beyond criticism lower than Ruskin's. But I am not any good at that. I am good at making a plodding response and, later, getting angry.

"It sold some copies," I said.

O'Malley waved his cigar as though it were a scepter. "Several stories involving Fresco Thompson and Buzzy Bavasi were unfortunate."

"They came off tape. I still have the tape. There aren't any eighteen-minute gaps."

"They were so unfortunate," O'Malley said, "that I asked my son Peter what in the world has gotten into our Brooklyn friend."

Ah, but we argued long ago in Brooklyn, too. O'Malley is a consistent man and he has consistently believed that the first function of the sporting press is to sell tickets to Dodger games. I looked out a window. O'Malley reigns in an office far down the left-field line. Unlike the couple in Pine Bluff, he does not have to hurry out to guard his windows. Jimmie Foxx, mightiest of righthanded sluggers, could not have driven a ball within thirty yards of Walter's windows.

The stadium seats are color-keyed. That means your ticket comes in the same shade as your seat. Blue is fair and green is good and red is splendid and yellow suggests not cowardice, but fame. The movie people vie for yellow tickets. Beyond all that lies Elysium, for the honored few: box seats, closed-in with Herculite, surrounding home plate just below field level.

One evening Elizabeth Taylor sat behind home plate. Décolletage cut deeply. "Wow," said John Roseboro, the catcher, in an earnest pre-game conference at the mound.

"I'll take care of you, buddy," said Don Drysdale, the pitcher.

Drysdale's first pitch that night was a medium-speed fast ball, thrown fifteen feet above Roseboro's head. The catcher sighed and trotted toward the backstop. Ms. Taylor sat perhaps a foot beneath him. John Roseboro had an extraordinary amount of difficulty picking up the ball. According to current baseball lore, Ms. Taylor is a true brunette.

That was the 1960s. This morning, of the '70s, Dodger Stadium lay empty. The aisles and seats had been swept clear of litter and gum, deposited by 52,469 customers the night before. Toward the right lay the ball field, green and white and a reddish tan. To the left, from O'Malley's office, lay hills that had been barren. They are irrigated and showed the green of watered pines.

"What a pleasant office you have," I said.

"Not so pleasant," O'Malley said. "Outside my window there's a grounds keeper standing in center field with a hose, and I wonder, if he's going to use a hose, why the hell did I put $600,000 into an underground sprinkler system?"

"Why *does* he use a hose?"

"Because we brought him out from Brooklyn and he used a hose there," the owner of the Los Angeles Dodgers announced, impatiently.

O'Malley and I go back four decades, not only to a single borough, but to a single neighborhood and to a single private school, long since destroyed by urban blight. "You know," O'Malley said, mingling sentiment and blarney, "I take pride in being the man who handed you a diploma when you graduated from Froebel Academy. You certainly looked at things more positively then."

Like Joseph Kennedy, or FDR, he is an indefatigable one-upman. Like them he is a master of his trade. That trade is major league baseball.

"You want to know about our success out here," O'Malley said. "Able to afford a private plane; our training complex at Vero doing so well. First, we're not a syndicate. The Dodgers are a family corporation. Second, we don't have absentee ownership. Third, the chairman of the board, with whom you're sitting and who isn't getting any younger, comes to work at 8:30 on the morning after a night game. When the board chairman shows up that early, the rest of the staff tends to do the same."

O'Malley approaches me with suspicion because I write, as I approach him carefully because he criticizes. Still, Fred Claire, the Dodger Vice President for Public Relations, set up a schedule of interviews which taxed my ability to assimilate and caused one cassette recorder to expire.

Like the International Business Machines corporation, the Los Angeles Dodgers are a cohesive organization, and like IBM people, Dodger officials follow a company line. Across a May week in Los Angeles, the line went like this:

We've been the best organization in baseball. (Probably.)

We're good because we work harder than anybody else. (Perhaps.)

We lost the 1975 pennant to Cincinnati because of injuries. (Nonsense. The Dodgers had no Johnny Bench, no Joe Morgan, no Pete Rose.)

"We just ran into some bad breaks," said Al Campanis, the general manager, a bulky, black-haired man of forty-nine. "And what the hell are you doing wearing a beard?" Campanis was born in Kos, Greece. I wanted to ask him what the hell Socrates was doing wearing a beard. But baseball people needle quite impersonally. Manners exist, but do not dominate. Pee Wee Reese, a paragon of geniality, sometimes greeted acquaintances, "Hello, Horse Shit."

I heard Al Campanis out on Dodger injuries, a courtesy that may have gone unnoticed. Or maybe not. For suddenly, with a Byzantine flourish, Campanis showed me his private treasury. Fourteen tapes of Branch Rickey lecturing on baseball. "Nobody else has this stuff," he said.

I remembered Alexander Sebastian Campanis as an ambitious man who worked with minor league players in 1952. He had earned a master's degree from New York University, and you could not know Al Campanis for ten minutes without hearing about it. (I knew Wally Moon for twenty years before he mentioned his M.S.) Campanis played seven games for the Brooklyn Dodgers in 1943 and hit two singles in twenty times at bat. During our first encounter, he confided that he had taught Jackie Robinson how to make the double play.

"Is that what he says?" Robinson asked one afternoon. "Well, tell him I guess I could have worked out the pivot by myself." Laughter shone in Robinson's eyes. He had been something more than a .100 hitter himself. "No.

Don't tell him. Al Campanis is a good guy. He was very good on integration when it counted."

In his large, amorphous office, Campanis offered me excerpts from the Rickey tapes.

"Thou shalt not steal," Rickey said. "I mean defensively. On offense, indeed thou shall steal and thou must."

Amid such platitudes lies baseball gold. According to Rickey, the change of pace is a magnificent pitch. Instruct young pitchers in the art of changing speeds. But first let them master a fast ball and control. Teach changing speeds in Double A, or Triple A. On tape Rickey suggests that pitchers will have gained confidence and sophistication at that level. Look for ball players who run and hit with power. Neither speed nor distance hitting can be taught. Consider the present and simultaneously plan for the future. Luck is the residue of design. Once Rickey assembled his ruling staff and cried out in the voice of Job, "I stand on a cliff. On the edge of an abyss. I lose my footing. I stumble toward the yawning gates of hell. One man can save me. Only one. I ask each of you, who is that man?" This meant the Dodger bullpen was uncertain. Rickey wanted a consensus on the best minor league reliever to recall. The name was Phil Haugstad, who won none and lost one.

Working with the Rickey legacy, but not the Rickey flair, Campanis is constantly fractioning baseball into component parts. Then he discourses in general terms on teaching incentive.

"History," he says, "is full of people who accomplished their goals after having had failures. A negative attitude slows reflexes and dulls perception. With a positive attitude you can find some good in failure. Thomas Edison was looking for a substitute for lead in storage batteries and his first twenty thousand experiments were unsuccessful. Somebody asked if he felt discouraged. Edison said nothing had been wasted. He'd found twenty thousand things that didn't work."

I moved to the dugout, where Walter Alston was waiting. Alston started managing the Dodgers in 1954 and that year brought a championship team home second. But a year later the Brooklyn Dodgers won the World Series. If you want to find someone with a lower lifetime batting average than Al Campanis, Smokey Alston, of Darrtown, Ohio, is your man. He came to bat once for the St. Louis Cardinals in 1936 and struck out. He never batted in a major league game again.

When Alston took over the old Brooklyn Dodgers, he was inward, suspicious and uncertain. He made mistakes. That spring the Dodgers were a set team, with veteran stars. Emphasizing, indeed overemphasizing, the function of manager, Alston insisted every position was open.

"I got a hunch I might just start at shortstop," Pee Wee Reese said with soft, angry sarcasm.

"Does he think now, after all these years, I'm gonna have to fight my way into the line-up?" Robinson said. "Son of a bitch."

At press conferences, Alston insisted that his line-up would not be determined until opening day and at length I telephoned Charlie Dressen, who had managed the Dodgers to a pennant the year before. "I'll give ya the opening line-up," Dressen said. I then wrote a deadpan story beginning:

"Charlie Dressen today announced the Dodgers' opening day line-up. Jim Gilliam at second will lead off. . . ."

The story exacerbated Alston's insecurity and for many years this large, stolid middle-American greeted me with a glower. But at sixty-five, as the oldest manager in baseball, he was mellowing. He offered a shy smile, called me by name and said that the old Brooklyn Dodgers had been generous. "They didn't know who I was and they could have made things tougher for me than they did." He had some pictures of his farm to show me and photos of his grandchildren. An elegiac quality ran through his talk.

"Are ball players very different today?" I said.

"I don't think so," Alston said. "I honestly don't. If I've changed my managing techniques much, I'm not aware of it. Hit and run. Cut-off play. The game's the same."

Someone was warming up without his baseball cap.

"Now that," Alston said, "would never have happened at Ebbets Field. I guess there're outward changes, facial hair and cassette players, but if you don't like some of these surface differences, you simply have to learn to look away. Below the surface ball players are ball players in the thirties and in the fifties and now. We've had three eras out west. Carl Furillo, Duke Snider and the rest were past their prime when they got to Los Angeles. Wally Moon helped the club. Next, a fast team, fine pitching, with Sandy Koufax, whose perfectionism I admire. Now this good team, Steve Garvey, Ron Cey and Davey Lopes. How long will I keep managing? It's always been a one-year contract. I wouldn't stay anyplace I wasn't wanted. I can teach school, you know. Used to do that in Ohio. But I'll make my decision next October. I make it every October. Meanwhile, I have a delightful job."

At the batting cage, Dixie Walker instructed Steve Yeager, a good young catcher, with side comments to Mike Marshall and me. As a batting-practice pitcher threw, Walker chattered caressingly, "Think opposite field, Steve. Think other way. They're going to give you outside sliders, Steve. No one can pull them. Don't worry about the other, the inside stuff. Your hands are so quick you'll pull everything there, the way Babe Ruth did. I played with Ruth."

Yeager popped three outside fast balls to right. Walker winced. Then he said, "I can't push him more. Ball players have changed. On the old Tigers, nobody told you anything. Only Charlie Gehringer—he wasn't a coach, but a player—said I should go the other way."

"You think this guy is working?" Mike Marshall said.

"I think so," Walker said. "But if I push him too hard— it's this new generation—he'll work against me. Against you."

Dixie Walker—Fred Walker from Villa Rica, Georgia— is a tall, courtly man who speaks with a soft high-pitched drawl. Working with Yeager, who is white, and with a black outfielder named Dusty Baker, he seemed first gentle and then extremely wise.

He talked about control, a pitcher's control, and how most of us say that a pitcher is wild when he throws a curve that bounces in the dirt. "But there's another kind of wildness," Walker said. "The pitcher wants to throw a curve down low and away. That's the good pitch. He throws it belt-high over the center of the plate. That's the home run. Visualize and you'll see that both pitches were just about as wild. They're equally off target. The difference is only in direction. But the second one, the home-run ball, is not the kind of wildness everyone picks up. People don't realize a man can be wild and throwing strikes."

I nod, amazed that I had never viewed control that way. It becomes obvious after Walker says it, just as it became obvious to use tungsten as a filament after Al Campanis' man Edison had lit his lamp. But Walker did say it. The applicable noun is "professionalism."

Long ago, when the Dodgers slouched toward the first division to be born, Dixie Walker appeared in Brooklyn as a hero. The year was 1940, and a generation of Dodger fans lusted for an outfielder, for anyone, who could hit. Dixie could hit. He drove in runs. The Dodgers won a pennant in 1941. Sportswriters from Manhattan, making one more patronizing Brooklyn joke, described Dixie Walker as "The People's Cherce." Cherce? Choice. The Dodgers had a star.

After World War II Branch Rickey hired Jackie Robinson and, unthinkable as it was in the liberal Democratic borough of Brooklyn, Walker asked Rickey to trade him, rather than make him play beside a fellow Georgia native who was black. Walker went. Robinson stayed. A year later, now hitting well for Pittsburgh, Dixie Walker retired.

About 1955, Walker explained painfully and unconvincingly that he owned a hardware business in Alabama and that having a black teammate could drive him to bankruptcy. Now in 1976 at Dodger Stadium, other players, some black, some white, appeared before him for instruction. Walker's paternal teaching tones reached out equally to everyone. Knowledge of pitching and hitting and teaching was not, I suspect, the highest mountain Walker had to climb. Rather it was achieving, as he had this day in his sixty-fifth year, absolute color-blindness on the ball field.

Chunky, ebullient Tom Lasorda said he wanted to manage the Dodgers. Lasorda was Walt Alston's third-base coach, and in the politics of baseball third-base coaches are supposed to pretend that they have found nirvana waving runners home. But Lasorda's enthusiasm exceeded his prudence.

We sat by a locker. "Sure I want to manage," Lasorda said, "but here, not somewhere else. I've had offers, three I guess. I had fifteen of these kids when I managed in the minors. Now I want to manage them right where they are."

"Do you have any commitment from the team?"

Lasorda's face, pudgier than when he failed to make the Dodgers twenty years before, screwed into a wince. "No," he said. "None. But listen to me, to how I feel.

"This is my twenty-eighth year with the Dodgers, the greatest organization in baseball. Cut my veins and Dodger blue will flow. When I die, I want it on my tombstone: 'Dodger Stadium was his address, but every ball park was his home.'

"Mr. O'Malley, the boss, heard that and once he called me into the press room in spring training. He had a whole bunch of the press in there. And he presented me with a marble tombstone and on it was my name and a heart and a drop of blood painted Dodger blue.

"I was elated. Here was the president of the ball club presenting me with a marble tombstone, and I told him I was so grateful I wanted to go on working for the Dodgers when I was dead. Mr. O'Malley looked at me quite puzzled, and I explained. Beside the tombstone, when I die, they can hang out the Dodgers' home schedule. Then when people are in the cemetery visiting loved ones, they can say, 'Let's go to Lasorda's grave and see if the Dodgers are at home or away.' "

He rose, a stocky man of forty-eight. He was not smiling. In a way Ring Lardner would have understood, Lasorda was telling me exactly how much he wanted to manage the Dodgers.

Steve Garvey, the Dodgers' best ball player, is intelligent, handsome and so accommodating that I later asked Vin Scully, the broadcaster, if he could be as nice as he appeared.

"He is truly exactly that nice," Scully said. "And he hits and he has a beautiful wife and lovely kids. In fact he's so nice some people who aren't so nice resent him for it."

Garvey sat in the dugout, fresh-faced and strong, and he asked if he could help me out. "I have a theory about the crowds," he said. "It's interesting to see the type of crowds we get." Garvey did not pause. He spoke without arrogance, but as one accustomed to attention.

"Now the Friday night crowd is the one that has anxiety built up. They've been working hard for a whole week. They're coming to get out. They've been caught on the freeways. If you have a good Friday night, the cheers are a few decibels louder. If you have a bad Friday night, the people are rougher." A quick warm smile. "Friday is no night to play badly. The fans will crucify you.

"Saturday. Date night. That's just about what it sounds. Medium. If the guy and the girl are getting along, they're with you. If he spills mustard on her skirt, it's something else.

"Sunday we play in the afternoon. The Sunday crowd comes out to take their kids and see the stadium and the mountains in the background and the palm trees. This place is gorgeous. On Sunday afternoons the people are positive. You really have to be cheating them out of their entertainment to hear a boo.

"Monday and Tuesday nights you get the fans who really know baseball."

"When do you like to play most, Steve?" I said.

He touched his chin. "Fridays," he said. "The Friday crowd is the best challenge."

The Los Angeles Dodgers win games. They make money. They are a rousing team to watch, and that leads back to one seventy-three-year-old man, in a glass-walled office, glowering at a distant figure costing him money behind a hose.

I don't think the Brooklyn Dodgers, a glorious and

profitable franchise, should have been moved twenty seasons ago. A strong Commissioner would have vetoed the transmigration, as contrary to the best interests of baseball. The West then could have opened logically, with nascent franchises wriggling toward victory in San Francisco and L.A. I don't blame O'Malley, a graduate of Culver Military Academy, the University of Pennsylvania and once a hustling lawyer, for trying to move above the American middle class. Ford Frick, the reigning Commissioner in 1957, was all elocution and putty. Frick is a pleasant, pensioned fellow who these days likes to discuss the sport of curling. Sweep, sweep, Ford Frick. Walter O'Malley, conniving, serious baseball man, one word is owed to you and your Los Angeles success. Congratulations.

"We have been fortunate, obviously so," O'Malley said in his office. "We hoped we knew what fans wanted in a stadium. Good parking. We could still have done more there. Reasonable prices. We held the line, not increasing prices at all, for eighteen seasons. Last year, because of the free agency potential and this endless inflation, our top seat went from $3.50 to $4.00. We try to keep within the image of baseball as a daily event, so a feller can come home and afford to bring his wife or kids or grandparents. Our demographic image is the best in sport. I see them coming in with canes, walking sticks and wheelchairs, and I see the middle generation and I see the kids. Everybody's getting a reasonably priced evening's entertainment. The kids mean that we're building future fans.

"We've stayed in contention. That's all anyone can do.

Injuries. We had a lot of injuries in 1975. Suppose the Reds lost Bench and Morgan? We stay in contention and we're the only team that ever has or ever will fly the World Series pennant on the Atlantic and the Pacific Coast."

He looks very much as he did twenty years ago. Round face, round spectacles. Dark hair. The same incredible alternation in expression between paterfamilias and trial lawyer.

"If they had built you a ball park in Brooklyn, would you have stayed?"

"I've got to correct you there. You're falling into the same trap the others have. A boy from Froebel Academy should know better than that." The cigar waves. Walter O'Malley shakes his head.

"I never asked them to build me a new ball park in Brooklyn. I said we would build it on taxable land with our own money. We had a site at Atlantic and Flatbush Avenues, where the subways intersected. There's no place back there big enough for many lots, so in those days I thought you could park your car at any subway station and come to the ball park for a dime.

"Now there was a thing in New York. Bobby Wagner was the mayor. A nice man, not very strong. I knew his father, the Senator. Robert Moses was the real power in New York.

"We had a site and a sports authority was set up to condemn the land we needed, but Bob Moses blocked us. He had a site of his own, bounded on one side by water, another by a cemetery, a third by slum and on the fourth by a parkway, which meant that everyone going to our games was going to have to pay out to Bob Moses' toll booths. I couldn't see us drawing much from the water or the cemetery. I was afraid there might not be too much enthusiasm for paying tolls to Moses. I saw a future of empty seats. We *had* to come out here. We had ambitious plans for Brooklyn. We were toying with a domed stadium. We were looking ahead to pay television and hoping to get some financing that way, but they wouldn't give us the land we needed.

"The writers have been snowed under by a theory that this L.A. thing was a big giveaway. This park was built for $22 million and it didn't cost the taxpayers a dime. If you want to consider the difference between private enterprise and socialism, look at our park here and the one the City of San Francisco built. Public monies wasted out there in the cold and wind of Candlestick Point.

"We pay the City of Los Angeles more than a million dollars in real estate taxes. They write we've got the oil and mineral rights to our land, and that's so much bunk also. If someone struck oil back of second base, the oil would belong to the City of Los Angeles."

He turned and gestured toward the hills behind center field. Chavez Ravine, once arid, had bloomed into a wonder of evergreens and desert plants. "Buzzy Bavasi, when he was working, asked me why I was spending all that money landscaping when we play six nights a week and nobody can see the hills after the sun sets. I told him I was doing it for our Sunday afternoon customers. You won't believe it, but growing things are important to me." Outside, beyond the man with the hose, 55,000 seats looked clean and beckoning for the crowds that would start driving up Elysian Park Avenue, after the sun had burned away the smog.

"We took a chance. They told us Los Angeles was not a baseball town. We had a short lease on the Coliseum and then we were at the mercy of the City Council. I think we won out there by a single vote. Otherwise we might have been playing in the street."

O'Malley glanced through the window again, sighed slightly and beamed.

"Even my son asked me why I was risking, by putting so much money into the ball park. I told him, 'Peter, after I'm gone and maybe after you are too, this ball park will remain and it will be a monument to the O'Malleys.' "

He turned back to his correspondence. "Is there anything else for now? Otherwise I'll see you at lunch."

Outside in a corridor I passed Peter O'Malley, a six-foot-three-inch graduate of the Wharton School, who has run franchises at Spokane and Albuquerque and now is president of the Dodgers, under the chairman of the board.

"How'd it go with Dad?"

"He doesn't know how to be dull."

"Where are you heading?"

"Houston."

Peter O'Malley shook his head. "That's scary, what's happened down there. Is it true the Astro operation is $33 million in debt?"

2

The Houston Astros, formerly the Houston Colt .45s, have played under six managers and four general managers since they were organized in 1962. That was the year the Mets lost 120 games for Casey Stengel.

In 1963, the Astros had a promising first baseman named Rusty Staub and a good-looking outfielder called Jim Wynn. They traded both. In 1964, as the Mets lost only 109, the Astros found an aggressive young catcher from San Antonio, Jerry Grote. He went to New York. In 1965, the Astros started a swift second baseman named Joe Morgan and employed Dave Giusti, a dogged relief pitcher with a palm ball. Giusti has since become a star at Pittsburgh. Morgan has twice won the Most Valuable Player award. He was playing for the Reds. The Astros have traded Cesar Geronimo and Jack Billingham to Cincinnati, John Mayberry to Kansas City and Mike Cuellar to Baltimore, where Cuellar won the Cy Young award, as the best pitcher in baseball.

Beyond such deals lies an eerie death book. Jay Dahl, a Houston pitching prospect of great promise, died in an auto wreck twelve years ago. Jim Umbricht, another pitcher, died of cancer at the age of thirty-three. Don Wilson, who had pitched two no-hitters, was found dead in a car beside his home in Houston in the wretched morning hours of January 5, 1975.

After this mix of error and disaster, the Astros went

bankrupt. When I reached Houston in May of 1976, the team was controlled by the General Electric Credit Corporation, the Ford Motor Credit Corporation and a finance company. "I'd like to own a ball club," I told Sidney Shlenker, a thirty-seven-year-old Houston banker and promoter, who was caretaker president of the team. "Thing is my check would bounce."

Shlenker, a large, soft-voiced, putatively amiable man, smiled. "The way things have been going," he said, "a bad check would be better than none at all."

To most of America, Houston symbolizes what remains of Lyndon Johnson's war-bought prosperity. Johnson looked on Texas as John Kennedy is said to have looked on each especially favored mistress. He took care of her.

Austin grew and Dallas grew and Midlands grew and Odessa grew and the Pedernales River became, if not the Hudson or the Nile, then at the least a Southwestern Potomac. Contracts, for war material and for spacecraft and computers, flowed into Texas. Everywhere jobs sprang up and bankers smiled. The hub was Houston, a boundless sprawl of a city, set on flatland and marsh, fifty miles northwest of Galveston, at the head of Buffalo Bayou, a tributary of Galveston Bay. Once the marshes were malarial. As late as 1961, when Houston entered the National League, visiting ball players complained about mosquitoes as big as vampires. "Some of the bugs there are twin-engine jobs," insisted Sandy Koufax of the Dodgers.

But with the coming of Lyndon Johnson and air conditioning Houston triumphed over its environment. The people had money. The area had seven decades of rich baseball history. Clark Nealon, a journalist and baseball historian, combines Houston boom and Texas baseball tradition into a paragraph:

"When Buff Stadium opened here in 1928," Nealon writes, "it was freely described as the country's finest minor league ball park. But Branch Rickey, who supervised the construction, was concerned that Buff Stadium was too far out of town. Today the stadium is gone and a huge furniture store occupies the site. And where is that furniture store now? Pretty much in the center of downtown Houston."

My own arrival at once suggested growing pains and imperfections. Houston Airport lies twenty miles north of the city limits and nobody seemed able to suggest a direct route to my hotel. It was night and I felt somewhat worn from my laborings among the Dodgers.

"All right," I told the woman at the auto-rental desk. "Just give me a Houston road map and I'll find my own way."

She showed a metallic smile that would have done credit to an airline hostess. "We don't have any maps of Houston, sir."

"What do you have a map of? Milwaukee?"

"I'll check with my supervisor," she said. I let it go. There was no map of Milwaukee, either.

The clerk at the Astroworld Hotel had no record of a reservation. "The ball club made it," I said.

"We're almost full up," he said. "We have a convention of high school bands, but I'll find something."

The room was small and overlooked a neon sign, which

blinked on-off, on-off through the drapes. On the wall facing the bed a painter had gone to great pains to make a tree, with branches blossoming into bats, baseballs and ball players. I turned out the light. The neon sign blinked on and off. I wondered when the high school bandsman in the next room would begin tuba practice. He never did, but a schoolboy above forgot to turn off a faucet. By morning my bathroom lay two inches deep in rusty water. "A splendid breeding ground," I told the room clerk, "for anopheles mosquitoes."

He growled an unrepentant growl.

"And now, I suppose, you're going to tell me that New York City is uninhabitable."

A year before, the Houston Astros had finished 43½ games behind the Reds, drawn 850,000 people and lost money. "When you get to Texas," suggested Wally Moon in Siloam Springs, "look up a fan called Herschel Maltz. He played ball with me at Texas A&M. A nonhitting Jewish first baseman."

We met at a pleasant restaurant, with dark oak tables and walls, off an enormous shopping plaza that was glassed in and air-conditioned and reminiscent of a comic-book vision of the future. Buck Rogers would have been comfortable jetting around that shopping center under the repeating glass arches, breathing air that had been precooled and predried.

Maltz, now president of Century Papers, Inc., confirmed that he was a first baseman, nonhitting and Jewish. "But I had a good glove," he said. "Real good. Did

Wally happen to mention that?" Then Maltz talked about Houston's boom, with a quiet, drawling pride.

"About the ball club," I said.

"I'm turned off," Maltz said. "I used to go to forty games a year. I'd take customers. This year I haven't been to the Dome once. You know, I've been thinking that maybe they ought to change the rules of baseball. Give it a quicker pace, make it more lively, like football."

Make it more lively is a euphemism for win the pennant. There were no yawns last October in New York or Cincinnati. Bringing a contender into Houston is the weighty charge of Talbot Smith, an intense, precise bespectacled man of forty-three, who had resigned as executive vice president of the Yankees to become general manager of the Astros in August of 1975.

"I come from New England and I don't dislike the East or even New York City," Tal Smith says. "We had a comfortable place out on Long Island. I certainly wouldn't have left that, and the Yankees, if I didn't think there was a challenge here and one that I could meet in the foreseeable future."

When, then, will the Astros bring a pennant race to their Dome?

Bill Virdon, the field manager, speaks. "It doesn't just depend on us. We're in the same division as the Dodgers and the Reds. How fast we can be competitive depends on what they do as well as what we do."

"We aren't trading away any more young talent," Smith said.

"Right now we're trying to get them to play hard, excit-

ing baseball," Virdon says. "Frankly, I don't see us competitive with the Dodgers and the Reds until the latter
part of next season at the earliest. But that's possible. I'm
shooting for it. And we're not finishing any 43½ games
out this year."

Texas was a promising land for major league baseball
when the Houston franchise was first organized. The state
was the birthplace of men who rose to baseball's pan-
theon, among them Rogers Hornsby and Tris Speaker. All
by itself, Texas once supported a Double-A minor league.
(Well, almost. Shreveport played in the Texas League,
too.) The old Houston Buffs were a top Cardinal farm.
Dizzy Dean began building his legend there.

"The Buffs were good and sometimes very funny," says
Clark Nealon. "They once had a right-fielder named Nick
Cullop, who played beside a fine center-fielder, Hal Epps,
who had one problem. Going for a fly Epps never shouted,
'I got it' or 'You take it.' He said he couldn't run and holler
at the same time. One night after a rainstorm Cullop and
Epps collided under a fly. Cullop ended on top with Epps
lying face down in a mud puddle. 'Now we're going to find
something out,' Cullop said. 'You can't say *I got it*. You
can't say *You take it*. Now we'll see if you know how to
say *Help.*'"

Texas baseball stories spring from seventy-five years of
tradition and Texas League anecdotes proceed at least
from June 15, 1902. That afternoon Corsicana defeated
Texarkana, 51 to 3. Old newspapers indicate that Texarkana used only one pitcher, a young man named DeWitt.
All by himself, DeWitt pitched a fifty-three-hitter. The

late J. Walter Morris, who had played shortstop for Texarkana, told why. The man who owned the Texarkana franchise, C. B. DeWitt, insisted to the manager, Cy Mulkey, that his own son be given a chance to pitch.

June 15, 1902, was the date on which Cy Mulkey yielded and started the boss' son. After young DeWitt had given up thirty-five or forty runs, someone suggested, "Why don't you take the kid out?"

"His old man said he wanted the kid to pitch and that's what the kid is gonna do. Pitch." Walter Morris used to muse that "On that day for that kid, giving up a double was a moral victory."

It was a Texas League manager who first devised an effective antidote to a spitball. The pitcher here, one Snipe Conley, was no DeWitt. He played briefly in the majors and once won nineteen consecutive complete games for Dallas. Late of a Texas summer sixty years ago Conley started an important game against the Wichita Falls Spudders. He began beautifully, the spitball dropping and lurching about home plate. In the third inning, Conley's tongue began to sting. An inning later the inside of his mouth burned and his tongue was swelling. He had to quit in the fifth.

A Dallas protest led into the Chemistry Department of Texas A&M. There technicians discovered that the baseballs had been coated with a clear derivative of creosote. Every time Snipe Conley put his fingers to his mouth to collect saliva, he was also applying an irritant. Nobody remembers whether the game was protested because nobody remembers whether creosote was illegal in Texas baseball sixty years ago.

Judge Roy Hofheinz, a bulky, aggressive Texas politician, won a major league franchise for Houston in 1961
with a few warm Texas baseball stories, a cold reference
to a Texas economic boom and a promise that he would
build a dome. "Considering Houston's heat, humidity and
rain," he said, "our best chance of success is with a wea-
therproof all-purpose stadium." The idea traces not
merely to Walter O'Malley's imagined pleasure dome for
Brooklyn, but clear back to the Roman Colosseum. When
it rained in Rome two thousand years ago, slaves worked
a series of winches that drew the velarium, an awning
probably woven from heavy Egyptian cotton, over the
top of the Colosseum. At the center, a hole, twenty yards
across, allowed for air flow. Since warm air rises, little rain
fell on the gladiators.

Hofheinz's dome, which opened in 1965, is described in
a brochure as the Eighth Wonder of the World. The Astrodome has almost three times as much space on the
arena floor as the Colosseum. It includes eating places
called The Countdown Cafeteria, The Trailblazer Restaurant and The Domeskeller. Skyboxes, available for about
$15,000 a year, adjoin club rooms, with telephones, ra-
dios, bars and furniture ranging from French Provincial
to Texas Gauche. In the VIP suite, five levels high, the
visitor can find an imitation medieval chapel, an imitation
sidewalk café and "the romantic Astrodome gazebo,"
while his children amuse themselves at the Astrotot Theater. The temperature under the dome is always 72 degrees, and paved parking areas surrounding the arena
provide space for more than thirty thousand cars.

As you walk toward the Dome in bad times for the

Astros, the parking lot stretches white and hot and barren of automobiles. Inside, the skyboxes are underoccupied. Within them, upholstery on both French and Texas furniture is wearing thin. Even the playing surface itself has become frayed.

But this is truly the original domed ball park, and if it is no longer what the brochure claims—"Space City's sparkling jewel"—it is still, in brochure English, a triumph of construction, engineering and electronic skills, all of which has nothing to do with winning a pennant.

Some sense of Roy Hofheinz's early business acuity came out of an Astroturf controversy. Originally, the field was sodded, under 4,596 transluscent plastic skylights, planned to let in enough sunlight to keep the grass growing. Unfortunately, all that translucence created a creamy backdrop against which it was impossible to follow a fly ball.

Hofheinz had the lucite darkened and began negotiating with representatives from the Monsanto Company to install artificial grass.

"We're thinking in terms of $375,000," a man from Monsanto said.

"You must be clairvoyant," Hofheinz said. "$375,000 was exactly what I had in mind to charge you for promotion for using your product in the dome. Take our name. Call it Astroturf if you like." The compromise gave Hofheinz what he wanted. An Astroturf ball field for free.

Baseball, Bill Veeck says, is a marvelous arena for jugglers, clowns and hustlers. On the surface, Hofheinz hustled to a poker player's taste. But behind the swagger, he lacked calculation, and, indeed, the caution that must come first. You will not win by calling with a ten-high hand unless you occasionally show your opponents a full house. You will not build the Dodgers or the Reds while concentrating on an Astrotot Theater.

Talking to a newspaperman, Hofheinz said that he personally possessed almost no money. "It just seems that way. I work with money that belongs to other people. That's the trick."

"You have more money than I do," the newspaperman said.

"Not in my own name," Hofheinz said. I cannot imagine Walter O'Malley operating with a bank account smaller than a newspaperman's. O'Malley could not imagine that, either.

The Houston Astrodome cost $38 million, which Hofheinz financed largely through $31.5 million in bonds, issued by Harris County, Texas. The current lease costs the Astros $750,000 a year. Then he built four hotels near the Dome, and a convention center called Astrohall and an amusement park called Astroworld, U.S.A.

The hotels were empty too often. The amusement park lacked the sparkling Disney touch. People came from fifty states to see the Dome. They arrived as tourists and did not become ball fans. The team kept trading its young talent, attendance slumped and on the fringes of Hofheinz's domain one heard the insistent whisperings of creditors.

In May, 1970, Hofheinz suffered a stroke. He now sits in a wheelchair, huge and bearded like Orson Welles, his empire suddenly revealed as a fiscal ruin. The four hotels and the convention center have been sold to Servico, a Memphis conglomerate whose executives talk of needing $2 million for renovations. Hofheinz's four hotels were undercapitalized. The amusement park has been leased to Six Flags Over Texas, and Ned DeWitt, president of Six Flags, says he'll have to invest $16 million to create a viable attraction. What I perceived of Hofheinz's Texas dream, then, was a ball park owned by the county, a ball club with some potential and a debt that Sid Shlenker conceded was "more than $30 million."

Along with empty seats, I saw good baseball at the Astrodome. The Astros played the Phillies tough in three fine games. Cesar Cedeno in center is a superb ball player. James Rodney Richard, the six-foot eight-inch right-hander, throws smoke. Roger Metzger, the shortstop, is fine. Greg Gross in left will get his hits. Virdon had his athletes working, and though they didn't beat the Phillies, they played them, in Virdon's term, competitively.

But it is premature to assert that the Astros' luck has turned. Tal Smith has introduced a promotion called The Foamer. On Foamer nights, a large bulb near a digital clock behind right field lights each even-numbered minute. Should an Astro hit a home run when the light is on, management buys one free beer for every adult in the house. As a chaser Tal Smith threw in something else. If Mike Cosgrove, the Houston pitcher, struck out Mike Schmidt when the light was on, that would be free beer for everybody, too.

At 9:12 Cosgrove got two strikes on Schmidt. He gazed

endlessly at catcher Cliff Johnson for a sign. The 17,338 fans made a rising inchoate noise. Finally, with the light still on, Cosgrove threw an inside fast ball. Mike Schmidt missed it. The crowd made an animal roar. Suddenly all over the Dome grown men sprinted up aisles. The place seemed to empty in seconds as the fans scampered toward refreshment stands.

In the sixth, with the Phillies leading 2 to 1, and men on first and third, Cosgrove walked the Philadelphia pitcher. Before the inning ended, the Phils had secured the game.

Talbot assumed a look of patient resignation. "With nobody on, he strikes out Schmidt and costs us $5,000 in beer. Then, with the game in the balance, he walks the pitcher." Smith laughed to himself. "We're turning a corner, but we haven't turned it yet."

Certain Houston business people assert that if Hofheinz had not been stricken, he might yet have rescued his empire. Interest on a $30-million debt demands respect, or rather awe, and I am less qualified even than the former comptroller of New York City to comment on multimillion-dollar juggling.

Houston's baseball disaster is something else. Caught in his measureless Texas dreams, Roy Hofheinz didn't pay enough attention to his franchise. Baseball is competitive on the field and baseball is competitive in the front office and perhaps, while Hofheinz mused about Astroworld, Bob Howsam of Cincinnati was talking to the scout who signed Johnny Bench.

No one has accused Walter O'Malley of dreaming small, but like every successful baseball executive, he keeps his focus: the diamond. The team has to win or come close.

Judged against an insurance company, a major league franchise is small business, and a big league franchise makes a weak base on which to build a financial empire. But looking after a franchise, with its farm teams, its scouts, its public relations, all the rest, is a full-time occupation for any executive.

The Dodgers are not for sale. "Does anybody ever try to buy them?" I asked O'Malley.

"About once a week," he said.

Peter O'Malley elaborated. "I'd say we average at least two serious offers a year."

Playing in the Eighth Wonder of the World, in air-conditioned Texas May, the Astros are for sale. As I flew out of Houston, the message from Texas was brief:

No takers.

3

The Country of the Poor

The president of the Eastern League, a round-bellied, hearty, country-slick New Englander named Paul Patrick McKernan, spends his winters teaching current events at Nessacus Middle School, outside the valley town of Pittsfield, Massachusetts. "I have a wife and four children," Pat McKernan says in the league office, which is the sunroom of his home. "Whatever you hear about a great American baseball boom, it doesn't apply here. The minors are a depressed area."

I have seen a list of salaries paid to major league baseball players during the season of 1975. These were not press-released exaggerations or newspaper guesses, but figures printed in a private analysis called "Salary vs. Performance." You can find copies within locked cabinets in any major league office, if you have either a jimmy or the right news source.

There are few surprises at the top. Excluding attendance bonuses and the variety of fringe benefits that materialized during Catfish Hunter's negotiations with the Yankees, Dick Allen led the majors. The Phillies had to pay him $250,000. Then came Hank Aaron at $240,000; Johnny Bench at $190,000; Lou Brock at $185,000 and Willie Stargell at $181,000. Although Aaron is the only lifetime .300 hitter in the bunch, every man here has been a superstar. Every man has been able to put customers into the park.

The highest-paid pitcher was Ferguson Jenkins ($175,000), not really that good any longer, but the Texas Rangers were desperate. Then came Tom Seaver at $170,000; Luis Tiant and Gaylord Perry at $160,000; and Steve Carlton and Don Sutton at $155,000. (On the advice of his tax people, Hunter limited his straight salary from the Yankees to $100,000. He will get deferred income for many, many years.) Whatever, here is a pitching staff most managers could tolerate.

I found the wages of lesser players truly startling. Fritz Peterson, an ordinary lefthander, earned $66,000 in Cleveland. His earned run average was 3.95. Bob Bailey, who began as a Wunderkind and grew up to be only a journeyman, earned $72,000 at Montreal. The average salary for major league pitchers in 1975 was $51,000. The average for players at other positions was $55,000. Either figure seems reasonable for six months of work in the most appealing of our games.

If you follow a basic law of economics—you can't pay what you don't have—these numbers suggested overall fiscal soundness in the major leagues. Add a television contract worth $50.8 million for the season of 1976, plus attendance running 10 percent ahead of the best previous year, and baseball assumed an emerald glow of affluence.

But travel to Pittsfield through the rolling Berkshire Hills and you find yourself in the country of the poor. In gentle New England June, when the Berkshire Brewers, Pittsfield's entry, led the Double-A Eastern League, a night game drew only 110 fans. Later the management imported Bobby Feller, "Rapid Robert" when nicknames were in flower, and the hardest thrower of his time. At fifty-seven, Feller has become a fine showman and he presented a splendid pre-game pitching clinic. The attendance at Wahconah Stadium was 351.

Pat McKernan sits up late analyzing what besets his minor league, but in Pittsfield one obvious and indefatigable monster stands against the sky. It is a master antenna for cable television. During certain evenings when the Brewers are at home, so is almost everyone else in Pittsfield. On one channel they can watch the Yankees. A second brings them the Mets. A third carries New England's summer demigods, the Boston Red Sox.

"The majors," Pat McKernan says, in his pleasant rambling home on Spadina Parkway, "recognize that we're necessary and wish to hell we'd go away."

"How about the big rich clubs?" I said. "Don't they try to help you out?"

McKernan's round face darkened. "They can be the worst." He mentioned one famous executive. "That guy wouldn't pay five cents to see Jesus walk on water."

"I know that guy, Pat," I said. "He happens to be Jewish."

"Then he wouldn't spend a nickel to watch Moses part the waters of the Red Sea," McKernan announced with finality.

Berkshire County in western Massachusetts mixes low hills, three-thousand-foot mountains, small farms, upland meadows, swift-running brooks. It is most famous now for Tanglewood, the Boston Symphony's summer retreat where a performance of Beethoven's Ninth draws fifteen thousand customers. But while Tanglewood is relatively new, local baseball tradition traces almost to Beethoven's lifetime. One hundred and fifty years ago, children played varieties of ball games in the Berkshire fields, and in 1859 Amherst and Williams played the first intercollegiate ball game at Pittsfield. The curve ball had not yet been invented. Amherst won, 73–32. When I was ten, I repaired to those hills and a progressive playground called Camp Robinson Crusoe, that lay near the historic village of Sturbridge. I forget the reigning juvenile psychologists of the era, but "progressive" meant that we were supposed to plan our days. Each morning the boys in the bunkhouse met and voted on what we wanted to do. The counselor's role was limited to counting hands. A boy named Shep Ginandes and I possessed a primitive skill at rigging conventions. We wanted to play baseball and we kept the troops in line and we did play baseball every sunny summer day.

"But I want to throw the javelin," a timorous boy

named Joey Coopersmith complained.

"That's a girls' sport," Shep Ginandes said, with great authority. "They'll think you're a sissy at the Saturday night square dance," I said. ("Progressive" also meant that we were allowed to fox-trot on Wednesdays and do-se-do on Saturdays—in short, put our arms around young ladies. Nothing we did in the idyls of those summers frightened us more.)

On the morning of Joey Coopersmith's rebellion, a counselor interceded with a surfeit of good will. While the rest of us played our daily game of ball, Joey Coopersmith tossed a javelin wildly down the left-field line. I was playing third. I can remember more pleasurable games.

Each summer built to a day when the best of us were allowed to play the counselors, old men of nineteen or even twenty. We had a fine little lefthander named Spike Edelstein, who threw hopping fast balls for five innings, after which he tired. Every year we'd go ahead by a run or two, and feel o'erweening pride. Then Spike would lose his fast ball and the counselors would score ten times. That night the mood in the bunkhouse would be bitter as wormwood.

Spike Edelstein's father was a rabbi and I told Spike once that his old man ought to pray for sixth-inning rain. That way the game would be official but concluded while we were still ahead.

"Mind your own goddamn business," Edelstein replied, with the affability common to losing pitchers.

Years afterward I took to returning to the Berkshire Hills, but for music or to plant white pines or to consider, lying on my back, how the shiny green of oak leaves blended so beautifully with a clear high August sky. The local papers treated minor league baseball casually. The thought of traveling to Wahconah Stadium for a Double-A game simply never struck me.

"That's one problem," Pat McKernan conceded. "The summer people don't really know we're here. Besides that, a lot of the local people travel to Boston or clear to New York for the big league games. But minor league ball can work here. It did for me."

In October, 1969, McKernan bought an Eastern League franchise for $1,000 and concluded a working agreement with the Washington Senators. The Senators, nobody's first choice, offered the only agreement he could get.

Under a standard Double-A working agreement, the major league club supplies uniforms, nineteen players, a trainer and a manager. Double-A salaries run from $2,500 to $8,000 per season. The local owner pays $150 a month toward the salaries of the nineteen athletes. The big league club makes up the difference and pays the trainer and the manager in full. The big league club also shuttles players in and out at will.

"So you don't control your product," McKernan said, "but I thought I had a chance. I was a manager type in college, and I did some sportswriting in Batavia, New York. I figured I knew baseball and I knew this town.

"I was not only the president of the Pittsfield Ball Club. In the beginning I was the sole employee. I started speaking. I sold some tickets. I placed some ads for the next season's program. Renting a bus was a big expense, so I went to a bank and borrowed money and bought a nine-teen-fifty-something model bus that still ran well. No, the bank wasn't difficult. They knew me. The bankers wanted baseball here. And if anything went wrong, the bank had the bus.

"We have seventy home dates and I'd try to come up with seventy promotions. All kids in free. All right. Some of them bring parents. The parents pay. Then once you've got people inside, you're selling them franks and Cokes and beer.

"In the four years I kept the team we always drew between 44,000 and 50,000 fans a season. That averages better than 500 a night. I never touched a dime of my own money and the team itself never once lost money, except sometimes I couldn't pay myself any salary.

"Then in 1974 the league presidency opened. I wanted it, so I had to sell the club. Forget the *Sporting News*. I took an ad in the *Wall Street Journal*. It went like this:

> Did You Ever Want to Own a Baseball Team?
> Now's Your Chance

I listed my phone number and I got forty responses. I sold the team for $45,000."

McKernan sipped a soft drink. "I made money with the team and I enjoyed it, so I have no sour grapes, but what do the big boys like Bowie Kuhn tell you they pump into the minors?"

"The figure they claim is $36 million annually."

"Well, right here, in the Eastern League, it costs the

clubs with farms, the Dodgers and the Yankees and the Brewers and the rest, $80,000 to $100,000 to support a franchise. But look what they get. We have eight teams stretched between Pennsylvania and Quebec, and we're a training ground. The big league people get to see if their prospects can play under hard conditions, after tough bus rides, day games following night games, under lights that may not be the greatest. We play 140 games, so they find out which kids have the stamina, who can play night after night after night. We end up with a championship series, three-out-of-five. They get to see young players react to pressure.

"They could help by giving us continuity. I mean keep the same teams in the same towns year after year. That would be underwriting losses a little more in the short run. I mean attendance in a town could have a three-year slump. But you'd build a continuity of interest and maybe do better over a decade. They could let kids play in the regions where they grew up. They actually resist that. They say playing before home folks puts too much strain on a boy. So now a lot of Pittsfield people look at the Brewers as a bunch of visiting Californians, who won't be here next year anyway. They'd rather watch local kids playing American Legion ball. The major leagues could also stop televising us to death."

Pat McKernan sipped his soda pop. Three small children, Patrick and Kathleen Anne and Michael, darted into the office of the president of the Eastern League, and fled. Sunlight, falling through an old maple, dappled the room. "Well, look around the ball park," McKernan said.

"They've got some talent. The manager, John Felske, is a fine guy.

"And remember this, I'm only thirty-five years old. I expect to get in the majors someday myself. And then I'll remember, I hope I'll remember, the way things are out here among us poor people."

A Korps of Mercedeses with M.D. plates were the first cars to arrive at the Pittsfield Country Club, on the morning of a "gala baseball breakfast." There would be a parade up South Street and around the Pittsfield Common, where an old sulky, painted red, serves as a popcorn stand. Bands would play and in the afternoon at old Wahconah Stadium, the first intercollegiate baseball game would be re-enacted by young collegians wearing the heavy flannel uniforms of 1859.

The town fathers were proud of their promotion. "The year 1859 fits in with 1776 and the Bicentennial," someone told me, with mysterious arithmetic. "You know we're a pretty well-off place with our big General Electric plant. They make transformers."

"But if GE ever moves," someone else said, "the whole town is going to find itself on welfare."

Two village elders, Bob Dillon, a retired postmaster, and Fred Fahey, a three-letter man at high school in 1927, had been working on this breakfast for a year. They had even lured Lefty Gomez, the superb old Yankee pitcher, from his northern California home to make a speech.

"I am responsible for Joe DiMaggio's success," Gomez began, over platters of scrambled eggs. "They never knew how he could go back on a ball until I pitched. All I ever saw of Joe on the field was the back of his uniform. I wouldn't have known what he looked like, except we roomed together."

Gomez was sixty-six and sure of his comic delivery. He has been telling his stories for twenty-five years.

"I'll admit I was the worst hitter ever," Gomez said. His audience included Congressman Silvio Conte, lawyers, realtors, dentists and young people from Williams and Amherst. "I was so bad," Gomez said, "I never even broke a bat until last year. Then I was backing out of the garage."

He waited for the laughter to ebb. "I guess the worst was when I was managing Binghamton and we had a first baseman there named Dick Kryhoski. I put myself into a game in relief, but there was a tough righthanded hitter up, so I figured I'd better go to my pick-off move. Now that was a beauty. I not only picked off the runner. I picked off Dick Kryhoski. My throw hit him right in the chest. As soon as it did, there was Kryhoski, my own first baseman, hollering at the umpire, 'Balk. Balk.' "

Laughter rose to a roar. When it was quiet again, Lefty Gomez said, "You've got to concede, it's hard to win for a team like that."

Droll, not quite believable stories. A glory of good baseball times. But nobody at the Pittsfield Country Club could tell me why the young men representing the Berkshire Brewers had not been invited to the gala baseball breakfast.

That afternoon, 2,500 people filled Wahconah Stadium

and saw Williams defeat Amherst, 13 to 12, in a game played under the Massachusetts rules of 1859. It was a pleasant entertainment, somewhat overlong, and downright dull beside an Eastern League game played in privacy the next day.

John Felske, the manager of the Brewers, is a powerful six-foot three-inch native of Chicago whose major league career spanned three seasons and fifty-four games. He is authoritarian without being cruel, organized, precise and convinced that professional baseball must be a discipline before it can be fun. Terry Ervin, one of his outfielders, had just been suspended for bumping an umpire, and Felske made sure that Ervin drew meal money during his suspension.

"Just meal money?" Ervin asked. "I don't get my pay?"

"That's what suspension means. You don't play and you don't get paid."

"Then when do I have to show up at the ball park?"

Felske rubbed a strong hand through his sandy hair. "Technically, when you're suspended we don't even have to give you meal money. I want you at the ball park because I want you working out."

"It ain't right," Ervin said, "having to work out without getting paid."

"Think of that," Felske said coldly, "before you bump an umpire again."

Felske is thirty-four and has seen some boyhood Chicago friends go to prison. "I don't make a big thing of it," he says, "but we can all go wild as kids. My baseball career has kept me from making really wrong turns. I've made

mistakes, like telling off Leo Durocher. That got me off
the Cubs in twenty-four hours. But nothing disastrous,
and my own little kids are coming along fine."

Felske has a strong pragmatic intelligence, and through
twelve years as a catcher in organized ball, he has men-
tally recorded managerial excesses. Once he played
under Pete Reiser, an outfielder of infinite talent who
destroyed his career by running head first into walls. By
the time John Felske played for him, Reiser was a sour
man who ragged at his players. After one particularly
unpleasant session, Felske went out and got the hits that
won a game.

"I only was on you," Reiser said later, "because it makes
you a better ball player." Telling the story Felske smiled
a hard smile. "Reiser got on me because he was a disappointed man. Both of us knew that, but I just walked
away."

At Palatka, Florida, Felske played for Hal Jeffcoat, who
spent twelve years in the major leagues. During that season, Jeffcoat was fired. He immediately called a team
meeting.

"Before I go," Jeffcoat said, "there's just one thing I
want you all to understand. None of you sons of bitches
will ever make the big leagues."

If you play for John Felske, you make practice on time
or pay a fine. You work out hard and play hard or else
you're benched. You find the manager present at the ball
park and absent from team parties. ("I can manage the
ball players. I don't know about the wives.") But if you
extend yourself, you'll be encouraged, not humiliated,

and if your joy is playing Jethro Tull songs full blast on the team bus, you'll still be tolerated, if not endorsed. "All I can say," John Felske shouted over a Tull tape on one trip in June, "is that it's a good thing for you guys we don't have a fine for bad musical taste."

Felske's most interesting prospect and most delicate problem was a bespectacled outfielder–first baseman named Danny Thomas, who was batting .368 when I reached Pittsfield. Thomas had hit sixteen home runs and he was making diving backhand catches that showed perfervid competitive intensity. "Danny comes from the Chicago area like me," John Felske said, "but from a background of real, hard poverty."

A year ago at Reading, an umpire named Greg Henley called a questionable double play against the Brewers. The Reading second baseman caught the shortstop's toss, dropped it, recaught it at his knees and threw on to get the man at first. Had he retained possession at second base? Was the lead man out?

Greg Henley thought he was. Danny Thomas disagreed. After the game Thomas waited for Henley to dress. Then outside the ball park, he crashed a right-hand punch into the umpire's face. Pat McKernan suspended Thomas for the season.

Only two or three of John Felske's fine Double-A players will make the major leagues. He mentioned Jim Gantner, a trim, quick third baseman whose hitting must improve. Generally, Double-A players are expendable. Some Milwaukee officials wanted Thomas released at once. Uncontrollable hotheads make poor prospects. But

Felske asked for another chance to work with Danny. The two have since held searching talks on youth, wildness and throwing away a possible major league career through insensate rage.

Now the Brewers were playing the West Haven Yankees in the close and exciting second game of a doubleheader. About two hundred people sat in clumps on wooden stands at Wahconah Stadium, under an ancient iron roof. No town fathers were there, nor any of the affluent realtors and lawyers and physicians who had crowded the baseball breakfast at the country club. One saw children, admitted for twenty-five cents, and grizzled men who had bought tickets with what was left of Social Security checks. The middle class and people of middle years were missing.

A cluster of girls sat screened by mesh behind home plate. Wherever you find ball players, you find clusters of girls. That is a fringe benefit of playing in the obscurity of the minor leagues. Cocktail waitresses and shopgirls seek you out, responding to stabs of early desperation and dreaming of a man who can lead them to a better or a different life. The girls rooted, each for her man, with squeals and squirmings, like high school cheerleaders. But they were three, or four, or five years out of high school. It is somber to see people, even people at twenty-two, trying so hard to act younger than they are or than they look.

An old man wondered if I knew that Pittsfield teams had sent Al Rosen, the third baseman, and George Scott, the first baseman, to the major leagues. I asked for other names. The man thought for almost a minute. "Lou Gehrig played in this park once, but he was with Hartford."

A Pittsfield girl who worked for $2.25 an hour serving precooked hamburgers said that she might visit "the player I go with, in the winter." Her long, strong-jawed face brightened. "He lives," she said, "in California." To her, California, the sawdust-hamburger capital of the cosmos, beckoned like the Plaza of St. Mark. To her, a second-string minor league catcher whose baseball career was closing down in his twenty-third year appeared as The Mysterious Stranger.

Beyond, the grass shone softly. Wahconah Stadium borders the Housatonic River, which keeps the grass bright green and sometimes floods the outfield. A green wooden fence bounded the field. I climbed up to the press box on the iron roof. It seated three.

Below me, the Brewers moved ahead. West Haven stole the lead. The Brewers tied the score. When the game went into an extra inning, Felske sent for Lee McLaurine, a small, intense relief pitcher who had not given up a run all season.

With one out, Dennis Irwin, the Yankee catcher, walked. Dennis Worth lined a single to center, but Kenzie Davis, the Berkshire center-fielder, threw out Irwin at third base. Both teams play hard, aggressive baseball. Worth took second on the throw. Garth Iorg singled to left so sharply that Worth had to stop at third.

Two out. Two on. Tie game. Pete Ward, the Yankee manager, thought briefly of pinch-hitting for Mike Fischlin, his shortstop, who was batting .198. For no reason

Ward could later explain, he decided to let Fischlin hit.

McLaurine threw a breaking ball and Fischlin looped it 135 feet down the first-base line. Neil Rasmussen, at second for the Brewers, ran and ran and dove and caught the ball one-handed. He fell hard on his left elbow and the ball popped out of his glove. His momentum had carried him yards into foul territory. Not he, nor Danny Thomas in right, nor Dave Lindsey, the first baseman, moved to retrieve the baseball. They all assumed Mike Fischlin's pop-up was foul.

But Ted Denman, umpiring behind home plate, gestured that the ball had been fair at the moment that it touched Rasmussen's glove. The West Haven Yankees kept running. The ball lay on the grass in foul territory. Worth scored. Iorg scored. Fischlin scored. You could not charge the second baseman with an error for his impassioned try. Mike Fischlin, a .198 hitter, had put the ball game out of reach with a 135-foot home run.

Three or four Brewers, but not Danny Thomas, stormed toward Ted Denman. John Felske, a big sandy-haired bear, sprinted from the dugout. He shoved several Brewers aside before they came close to the umpire. McLaurine, his game lost, his perfect earned-run average ruined, screamed in scarlet rage. Felske grabbed McLaurine's uniform and spun the pitcher ten feet away from Denman. Then, with his players blocked by his body and his authority, Manager John Felske lectured at Umpire Ted Denman until he ran out of words.

After the 9-to-6 defeat, Felske remained speechless with anger and disappointment for five minutes. We sat in the clubhouse sipping beer. "What did you think?" he asked me, finally.

"I didn't have a good angle on the ball, but what I think is, it was fair. The umpire said it was, and under the rules of baseball, that means it *was* fair."

"Hey, get this straight," Felske said. "I'm not questioning Denman's integrity. He called it as he saw it. I just believe Denman saw it wrong."

Most of the Brewers showered, dressed silently and departed. At length only Felske, McLaurine, Danny Thomas and I sat with our beers in the old wooden clubhouse. By now McLaurine's customary good cheer had returned.

"You know," he said, "I got so mad out there I was actually going to take a swing at Denman."

Danny Thomas, last year's Reading wild man, sat up straight. "Lee," he said, "don't you *ever* do that. Curse, if you got to. Throw your cap. Kick dirt. But never hit an umpire. It just isn't worth it, and think about it, will you? It just doesn't make any sense."

Felske gazed at me across a beer can. I have never seen a manager's face shine with greater pride.

It didn't matter then to John, only to me, that for this, the most exciting game I'd seen on any level all year, only two hundred people sat in the grandstands of Wahconah Stadium, hard by the Housatonic River, in the old New England valley town called Pittsfield.

4

Golden Triumphs, Tarnished Dreams

1

Although Artie Wilson's name appears in the 1974 edition of *The Baseball Encyclopedia,* the listing is cursory and the type size approaches invisibility. This abridgment of Wilson's record was intentional, but not malicious. To qualify for a full listing in the encyclopedia, a player must have had twenty-five turns at bat in the major leagues. Artie Wilson, one of the finest shortstops baseball has known, came to the plate twenty-one times for the New York Giants of 1951. His big league career was a brevity of pathos.

The cavalier way in which Wilson has been treated says something about what is supposed to be baseball's fundamental reference work. It says more about the game itself, which prevented Wilson and generations of players like him from qualifying for the encyclopedia for a single and, indeed, malicious reason. Artie Wilson is black.

When you dig further, the records on Wilson still yield only a fraction of his truth. He played shortstop, second and first with the Giants, and batted .182. Officially Wilson was thirty during his major league season. Some suggest he was four years older. Whatever, his skills had long since been eroded by having to play professional baseball eleven months a year to support himself and his family. Monte Irvin, who was thirty-one himself before he was allowed to begin a splendid eight-year adventure in the majors, says, "Artie was a superstar before the term was invented. In the old Negro leagues we called him The Octopus, because it seemed as though he had eight arms. He had tremendous range, wonderful speed, a superarm. Beside that he was a first-rate punch hitter, always on base, always making trouble for the pitcher. But by the time they let him join us on the Giants, he wasn't the ball player we'd known."

I found Artie late in June among the damp green silences of Portland, Oregon, where his minister, the Reverend Thomas L. Strayhand, says no racial problems exist. Pastor Strayhand smiles slightly. "That's because there aren't enough of us blacks here for them to notice."

Wilson sells Chryslers on commission for a company called Gary-Worth, and through three rich days together he managed to mention in his quiet, relaxed way all the merits of a model called the Cordoba. Artie is a hard-working auto salesman and, yes, I would buy a used car from that man. But mostly we talked baseball, which Wilson looks back on with a warmth that others focus on distant, old romances.

"Oh, but I loved playing the game," he said in the tidy living room of his two-story white frame house in northeast Portland. "I loved it as a little kid round the sandlots in Birmingham and I loved it playing for the Acipico Cast Iron Pipe Company. Say, you know I played against Willie Mays' daddy back then. Cat Mays played for Westfield in the Tennessee Coal and Iron League. He could move, but he didn't have big hands like his boy. I loved it with the Birmingham Black Barons. We used to have an All-Star game in the colored league. I was the starting shortstop. Long about the fifth inning, they'd let Jackie Robinson come in and relieve me. Jackie Robinson. He was my substitute."

Wilson is a trim, tidy man with a pencil mustache and a soft tenor voice. "I never thought Robinson had a big league shortstop's arm," I said.

"Right," Wilson said, "but Jackie cheated. He studied the hitters good and made up for the arm by playing position. He knew where they'd hit. Alvin Dark done the same thing for the Giants. There wasn't nobody who saw me and Jackie in 1945 who wouldn't tell you but one thing. I was the best shortstop. There isn't nobody with intelligence who wouldn't tell you something else. For integrating baseball, he was the best man."

Usually a ball player's home glares with trophies, placards and awards celebrating his triumphs. The first thing one noticed on entering Jackie Robinson's flagstone mansion in Connecticut was the silver bat he won for leading National League hitters in 1949. At Mickey Mantle's contemporary ranch, off a cul-de-sac in Dallas, the walls of one room blaze with color. They are bright with framed magazine covers, *Life, Look, Newsweek* and the rest. From each cover Mickey Mantle's visage stares.

"Where are your trophies?" I said to Artie Wilson. Only religious paintings hung in the living room.

"Around," he said.

"Can I see them?"

"But not around here. I gave some to my boy. He's a college graduate. He coaches sports in Hawaii. My daughter got some. She works for the conservation department of the state. But to tell you the truth there aren't all that many. The colored leagues, you know, they wasn't giving too much away. That's how they was. I ain't complaining. I liked being there."

What Artie loved was his one season playing for Leo Durocher and the Giants. "Leo had the greatest tricks," he said. "He'd carry a rubber cigar—he didn't smoke—and he'd come up to some rookie and say, 'Hey, gimme your matches.' Twenty minutes later he'd be asking the kid what he was doing in the Thunderbird Club last night. The rookie wondered how Leo knew where he'd been drinking. Leo had looked at the matches, that was how. But after a while the rookies got smart. You can't stay dumb forever. They stopped carrying matches and bought cigarette lighters. Then Leo would come up with something else. You couldn't get ahead of that man."

Putting his children through college meant that Wilson

had to supplement his income by playing Caribbean winter ball. "The guys I knew in baseball," he said, softly. "Luis Tiant's father down in Cuba. Best lefthanded pick-off move I ever saw. Silvio Garcia, an infielder. Durocher said he'd been worth a million if he was white. Luke Easter. They spoiled him up in Cleveland by getting him to pull. If they left Easter alone, he'd hit 'em 450 feet to any field. Would you believe there was a catcher in the Negro League who was the fastest man behind the plate I ever saw?"

"Josh Gibson?"

"No. Poor Josh went crazy and he died. Ol' Josh hit the longest homers I ever saw. This catcher's name was Lockett, and he could run so fast that going to back up first he'd beat the runner there. One day somebody hit a ground ball toward the hole and the pitcher forgot to cover. But the guy was out on a play that went from the first baseman to Lockett."

I thought of Satchel Paige's tall tale about Josh Gibson swinging so hard in Pittsburgh one day that the baseball simply vanished, heading east. A day later Gibson was at bat in Philadelphia, when the center-fielder suddenly ran backward, leaped and caught a baseball. According to Paige, the umpire looked at Gibson and announced, "You're out in Pittsburgh yesterday."

"I might believe your Lockett story if I saw it in a record book," I said to Artie Wilson.

"Can't," he said. A smile flickered, semi-teasing, semi-sad. "There ain't no records. It's like that game was never played."

Wilson did lead the Pacific Coast League in batting

once, and when he finds out that you know of that, he beams. "Oh, I was finishing up then. It wasn't like I had my real good speed. But I still could hit any Triple-A pitcher. I played for Charlie Dressen down at Oakland. He was a sharp one also, almost like Durocher. But not quite. Leo was off there by himself.

"Why, one time with the Giants, Leo came into a Pullman car where a lot of his ball players were shooting craps. Leo took off his jacket, got down on the floor and in half an hour he had every dollar in that Pullman. Then he stood up and told the players, 'You already been taken to bed. Now it's time for you to go to sleep.' " The memory made Wilson laugh softly in delight.

He grew up in black poverty outside of Birmingham, Alabama, but he says neither poverty nor segregation bothered him as a child. "I didn't know nothing else, and I was happy long as I could get into a game. For a baseball, we'd find an old golf ball somebody had hit out of bounds. We'd wrap some string around it tight and have our ball. For a bat, we'd saw down a tree branch. When I needed a buck or two for sneakers, I shined shoes.

"I was just naturally happy, long as I played ball. I got a job cutting pipes and playing for the Acipico Company team, and one day I got careless in the factory and lost part of my thumb." He showed me his right hand. The thumb was cut off at the knuckle. "Didn't hurt much and I just had to adjust my throwing a little. I pitched once in a while. In the colored leagues you had to play every position. After the accident I could make my fast ball move better.

"With the Black Barons we had an owner who ran a funeral parlor in Memphis. He paid us regular. We went from town to town by bus, always playing, which I loved, and I got so I slept better sitting up in a bus than in a bed. Then Abe Saperstein got the club and took us out barnstorming and we won every game we played. When we got back to San Francisco, Abe wanted to take us to Joe DiMaggio's Restaurant on Fisherman's Wharf. Then he got the word. A colored ball team wasn't welcome. I think that got me as mad as anything ever did."

Integration moved slowly. First Robinson. Then Larry Doby. Then Dan Bankhead. It was 1960 before the majors were truly open.

"But the years you were excluded from organized ball," I said.

"You're thinking now, not then. Then, like I say, I was just happy to be a professional baseball player anywhere."

Wilson drove me about Portland, soft-selling his Cordoba, pointing out the Civic Stadium, where the Portland Timbers were playing soccer, and the Columbia River, crowded not with salmon but with freighters. "Rains a lot and it's cool, but it's been my home for sixteen years. You have any plans for tomorrow?"

"No."

"Well, if I'm not intruding on you and interfering with your sleep, I'd like you to be my guest at church." It was a hesitant, strangely poignant invitation.

"Thanks," I said. "Appreciate that," I said. Then musing aloud, "Is your church integrated?"

"Of course it's integrated," Wilson said.

I attended Sunday school class at the Allen Temple Christian Methodist Episcopal Church, where we read II Corinthians and men debated whether sin began with taking a drink or getting drunk. The issue lay in doubt when services began. A youth choir sang "Come, Thou Almighty King." Wilson, Finance Chairman of the Allen Temple Christian Methodist Episcopal Church, supervised the passing of collection plates. Pastor Strayhand preached and chanted on life's decisions. Then he introduced a new parishioner, a portly man, gray-haired and short of breath. "Come sit up front, brother," the minister said. Artie Wilson found a straight-back wooden chair and placed it before the pulpit. The old man made his way forward, panting and wheezing, on a cane.

"You know our tradition," Strayhand said. "We greet new members of our church the second time they're here. But you can see the brother's condition. We never know when the Lord will summon one of us. I think we better greet this brother now."

The churchgoers ordered themselves into a line. One by one they shook the old man's hand and bade him welcome. The choir sang "Abide with Me."

After services, we gathered in the basement for a lunch of fried chicken, corn on the cob and hot apple pie. As they had for the old man, scores of people approached to shake my hand. All were black.

At dinner, Artie Wilson said, "You remember when you asked if my church was integrated."

"You told me it was."

"What I meant was that God don't know no color."

Then we were back to baseball again. Artie asked me what was happening in Seattle.

"Well, they have their dome, and Danny Kaye and Les Smith have the franchise and for the first few years the team there will be terrible."

"Is there any chance they might hire Leo to manage?"

"Depends on Durocher's health and how he's been getting along with Kaye. What makes you ask?"

The soft voice grew even more quiet. "I know a lot about the game. I can teach good. I'm fine selling cars, but I was just thinking that maybe if Leo got the managing job he might just happen to remember me."

The old Negro All-Star shortstop looked out a restaurant window into twilight. "My children has grown fine," he said. "My wife's a lovely woman. I'm at peace with myself. But I didn't just love *playing* that game. I loved being around baseball. The big leagues is the greatest baseball in the world.

"I don't miss nothing and I don't resent nothing, 'cept DiMaggio's Restaurant. But now at my age, if Leo got Seattle and hired me as one of his coaches, I could help him and be back in the major leagues again.

"I'd pray for that," Artie Wilson said without sadness, " 'cept you just shouldn't ask the Lord for too much."

2

Outside the multipurpose stadium in St. Louis, a hundred yards past the vaulting shadow of the Gateway Arch, a hulking statue purports to represent Stan Musial at bat. It is a triumph of ineptitude over sincerity.

St. Louis baseball writers who had watched Stan Musial play baseball for almost a quarter of a century engaged a sculptor named Carl Mose to cast Old Number Six in bronze. Then Ford Frick composed an inscription for the pedestal:

> Here stands baseball's perfect warrior.
> Here stands baseball's perfect knight.

The shoulders are too broad. The torso is too thick. The work smacks of the massive statuary that infests the Soviet Union. It misses the lithe beauty of The Man.

"I saw the sculptor when he was working on it," Stan Musial said, beside his pedestal. "I told him I never looked that broad. He said it had to be that broad because it was going to be against the backdrop of a big ball park. He missed the stance, but what kind of man would I have been if I'd complained? The writers were generous. The sculptor did his best. Look, there's a statue of me in St. Louis while I'm still alive."

A pregnant woman, armed with an autograph book, charged. "Write for my son Willie," she commanded. Musial nodded, said, "Where ya from?" and signed with a lean-fingered, practiced hand.

"Thank you," the pregnant woman said. "Willie is coming soon. After he gets here and learns to talk, I'm sure he'll thank you, Mr. Musial."

Inside the round stadium, the St. Louis Cardinals were losing slowly in wet July Mississippi heat. The final score would be Cincinnati 13, Cardinals 2. We had left after the fourth inning, when baseball's perfect knight passed his threshold of anguish at bad baseball played by the home team.

To reach most old ball players, even millionaire old ball players like Hank Greenberg, you simply call their homes toward dinner time. A pleased, remembered voice comes through the phone. "I had a good day playing tennis. How've *you* been? Who've you been seeing? Say, if you're in town, come over and we can talk about the old days."

To reach Stan Musial, you call the office of the resort and restaurant corporation called Stan Musial's & Biggie's, Inc. When I did, a secretary said politely but crisply, "I'm sorry. Mr. Musial is on a good-will tour of Europe. He'll be back briefly in two weeks. Then he's flying to the Montreal Olympics. We'll try to fit you in, but could I have your name again and could you tell me what this is in reference to?"

It was in reference to one thing. Stan Musial, neither a perfect warrior nor any sort of knight, is my particular baseball hero. I heard a teammate who knew him well call him a choker. "Considering his ability, he didn't drive in enough runs," the man said. Echoes reached Musial, who would not stoop to make a response. Across his twenty-two years with the Cardinals, Musial batted in a total of 1,951 runs. That number is so large as to be meaningless, except that it is the fifth highest total in the history of the major leagues. According to Jackie Robinson, Musial remained passive in baseball's struggle to integrate itself. "He was like Gil Hodges," Robinson said. "A nice guy, but when it came to what I had to do, neither one hurt me and neither one helped." But in 1972 Musial worked quietly for the election of George McGovern as President. He is a political activist, and on racial questions he favors the men Robinson almost certainly would have preferred.

Musial is a man of limited education, superior intelligence, a guarded manner, a surface conviviality and a certain aloofness. He knows just who he is. Stan Musial, Hall-of-Famer, great batsman and, thirteen years after he last racked a double to right center field, still an American hero.

We were rambling about baseball in one of his offices in St. Louis, when my wife, who can be more direct than I, interposed five questions.

"By the time you got to be thirty-five," she said, "and your muscles began to ache, did you still enjoy playing baseball?"

Musial nodded, touched his sharp chin and said, "I always wanted to be a baseball player. That's the only thing I ever wanted to be. Now figure that I was in the exact profession I wanted and I was at the top of that profession and they were paying me a hundred thousand dollars a year. Yes. I enjoyed playing baseball very much right up to the end of my career."

"About politics?" Wendy said.

"I'm a Democrat. Tom Eagleton, the Senator, says he remembers sitting in my lap when he was a kid visiting our spring training camp years ago."

"What do you think of Jimmy Carter?"

Musial laughed to himself. "I'd have to say he's very unusual for a candidate."

"You worked for Lyndon Johnson?"

"He asked me to run his physical-fitness program, and I did. I believe in physical fitness. I'm fifty-five years old and I still swim two or three hours every day."

"But didn't you find Lyndon Johnson vulgar?" Wendy said.

Musial looked at me impersonally, then at my wife. "No," he said, "because we only talked politics."

If I read him correctly, Musial had said in quick succession that Wendy's first question was naïve, that Carter was a prince of peanut growers and that Lyndon Johnson would have sounded obscene in a roaring dugout. Just as he hit home runs without seeming to strain, Musial had implied all these things without a suggestion of rancor.

People were always mistaking his subtlety for blandness. An agent employed by both Musial and Ted Williams once said, "If you want to make some money selling articles, stick with Williams. The other feller's nice, but there isn't any electricity to him." Then an editor at *Newsweek*, where I was working, directed me to prepare a cover story on Musial. "Pick up the Cardinals out in Pittsburgh," the editor said, "and make Musial take you to Donora. It'll work well, putting him back on the streets of the factory town where he grew up."

At Forbes Field, Musial said that he was driving to Donora the next day and I was welcome to ride with him, provided I agreed not to write about the trip.

"Why not?"

"I promised someone I'd visit sick kids in the hospital. If you write that, it'll look like I'm doing it for publicity. Then, my mother lives above a store. That's where she

wants to live. We had her in St. Louis, but she missed her
old friends, so she went back home and found a place she
liked. No matter how you write that, the magazine can
come out with a headline: 'Stan Musial's Mother Lives
Above a Store.' "

"Well, I have to come back with a story."

"We'll spend some time," Musial said, "and maybe get
something."

We talked batting, for three afternoons. To break a
slump, he hit to the opposite field. He remembered a day
at Ebbets Field when he had gotten five hits, all with two
strikes, and he remembered a year when he suffered
chronic appendicitis and played 149 games and hit .312.
He remembered the double-header at Busch Stadium
when he hit five home runs. He could even recall the
different pitches that he hit.

"Do you guess at the plate?" I said, finally.

The sharp-featured face lit. "I don't guess. I know."
Then Musial spun out a batting secret. He had memorized
the speed at which every pitcher in the league threw the
fast ball, the curve, the slider. He picked up the speed of
the ball in the first thirty feet of its flight, after which he
knew how the ball would move as it crossed home plate.

About eighty pitchers worked in the National League
then. Musial had locked the speed of some 240 different
pitches into his memory. I had done my work, asked the
right question, and Musial responded with a story that was
picked up by a hundred newspapers.

They oversimplified, as newspapers often do. "MUSIAL
REVEALS HIS BATTING SECRET"—as though one magic

trick could make us all .300 hitters. Even if you or I can identify a specific pitch thirty feet away, we are left with one-fifth of a second, the quickness of a blink, in which to respond. Musial's lifetime batting average, .331, did not trace to a single secret. It was fashioned of memory, concentration, discipline, eyesight, physical conditioning and reflexes.

Going for his three thousandth hit, Musial neglected to concentrate. The pitch fooled him and he took his stride too early. But he kept his bat back, as all great hitters do. With no batting secret, only sheer reflex, he slugged a double to left.

Under autographed photos of John Kennedy, Lyndon Johnson and Bob Hope in his office, Musial at fifty-five looked much as he did fifteen years before. The same surprisingly thin wrists. The same powerful back. A waistline barely thicker than it had been. The deceptive self-deprecation also persists.

"I'm semiretired," he insisted, but twice he broke off our interview politely to take business calls. Stan Musial's & Biggie's, Inc., a family-held company, owns two Florida hotels and a restaurant and a hotel in St. Louis.

"Are you a millionaire like Greenberg?" I asked.

"Just write that I'm not hanging for my pension. See, a long time ago, I knew I couldn't hit forever and I didn't want to be a coach or manager. So Biggie Garagani, who died young, and I started the restaurant in 1949. Biggie knew the business and I knew that just my name wasn't enough. I put in time. I like mixing with people up to a point and my being here was good for business. I still walk around the place six nights a week when I'm in town. So while I was playing, I was building a permanent restaurant business, and that just led naturally into the hotels. What's my title? President of Stan Musial's & Biggie's, Inc."

Self-made men from poor backgrounds often drift toward such politicians as Reagan, a self-made man from a poor background. Musial's liberalism developed out of decent respect for others, and has seemed to deepen as he ages.

"I don't think Polish jokes or Jewish jokes or black jokes are really funny," he said. "My dad came out of Poland and worked like hell all his life and what was funny about that? Pulaski came out of Poland and helped out in the American Revolution. Was that a joke? I've just come back from Poland and I enjoyed the country, the people and seeing them work hard building high-rises. Some of them knew me. I brought my harmonica along and played a little."

"Polish songs?"

"Yeah. Like 'Red River Valley.'"

At the ball park, fans flooded toward his box demanding autographs. It was a Sunday and the autograph board flashed messages welcoming groups from Alton, Illinois, and Springfield, Missouri. Before the Dodgers went to California in 1957, the Cardinals were the only major league team based west of the Mississippi, and they drew fans from Oklahoma, Kansas, even Texas. The new major league teams, Kansas City, Texas and even Houston, have chipped the Cardinals' huge regional base. But some of the people who approached Musial in the swelter of Busch Stadium wore overalls. They were farmers, and their families had rooted for the Cardinals by radio and then by television, in lonely white houses set far away among the prairies.

Now the Cardinals, like the city of St. Louis itself, were struggling through change. Bob Gibson had retired and Joe Torre had been traded and Lou Brock had edged past thirty-five. The new talent was inferior. Someone lined a single to right and the ball bounced over Willie Crawford's head.

"It's tricky playing that artificial surface," Musial said. "The ball hops high."

"Crawford plays out there every day," I said. "This is the major leagues." Musial winced.

More farmers and children extended scorecards to be signed. "Okay, let's wait for between innings," Musial said. "Give a fella a chance to watch a game."

Someone said, "Sure." Another clutch of fans arrived. Silent now, Musial kept signing.

The St. Louis ball park, called Busch Stadium, looks very much like Fulton County Stadium in Atlanta, Riverfront Stadium in Cincinnati and Three Rivers Stadium in Pittsburgh. Vast, white, concrete and circular, designed to accommodate both football and baseball and so ideal for neither. Each old ball park, Forbes Field, the Polo Grounds and Ebbets Field, possessed a special character, and a man watching a ball game knew at once where he was. The new modular arenas suggest neither history nor place, only efficiency. With McDonald's Hamburger

stands and Holiday Inns, they are part of the homogeniza-
tion of America.

Brochures advertising St. Louis as "The Gateway to the
West," boast of The Arch, a mighty curve of steel that rises
630 feet above the west bank of the Mississippi. (Gordon,
my older son, studying architecture at Columbia, describes it as "the ultimate McDonald's.") The Arch, the
new ball park and a restaurant called The Spanish Pavilion were expected to stimulate building in downtown St.
Louis. The idea failed and The Spanish Pavilion went
bankrupt. For miles west of Busch Stadium one sees drab
institutional housing, empty lots, decay.

"St. Louis is getting like Los Angeles," I complained to
Musial. "I can't seem to find downtown."

"It's the suburbs," Musial said. "That's where the shopping centers have moved. Downtown's a problem everywhere, isn't it? When I wanted a hotel here, I bought one
near the airport."

The Reds were six runs ahead. Fans continued swarm-
ing toward us. Still signing, Musial singled out Pete Rose
for praise and said he felt embarrassed that so many major
leaguers were hitting in the .200s. "There's no excuse for
that. You know why it happens? They keep trying to pull
everything, even low outside sliders. And you can't do
that. Nobody can. If you're a major league ball player, you
ought to have pride. Learn to stroke outside pitches to the
opposite field. That's part of your job. A major league
hitter is supposed to be a professional."

"Do you miss playing?" I said. Pete Rose rapped a single
up the middle.

"No," Musial said. "Nice stroke, Pete. I quit while I still enjoyed it, but I put in my time. I like to travel now, but not with a ball club. Have you ever seen Ireland? Do you know how beautiful Ireland is?"

Later we drove back to his restaurant; a crowd surrounded Musial in the lobby. He said to each, "How are ya? Where ya from?" One fiftyish man was so awed that he momentarily lost the power of speech. He waved his arms and sputtered and poked his wife and pointed. Musial clapped the man gently on the back. "How are ya? Where ya from?"

Musial had spoken to him. The man looked as if he might weep with joy. At length he recovered sufficiently to say a single word. "Fresno."

We found a quiet place to drink. "Does this happen all the time?" I asked.

"Isn't it something?" Musial said. "And I'm thirteen years out of the business. Say, you know what Jack Kennedy said to me once? He said they claimed he was too young to be President and I was too old to be playing ball. Well, Jack got to be President and two years later, when I was forty-two years old, I played 135 games and I hit .330."

"Ebbets Field, Stash," I said. "They should have given you the right-field wall when they wrecked the place. You owned it, anyway."

"What do you think my lifetime average was in Brooklyn?" Musial said.

"About .480."

"It only seemed that way," he said, in a gentle putdown.

"Actually, my lifetime average there was .360."

I can't imagine Galahad, the perfect knight, as a baseball hero. He was priggish and probably undersized. Which doesn't matter. Having Stanley Frank Musial is quite enough.

3

On January 19, 1972, Early Wynn, the pitcher, was voted into the Baseball Hall of Fame. Such tidings generally lead to a phone call from a wire service reporter, who asks the ball player for comment, and if you follow that sort of thing, you know what happens next. In a wash of sentiment, the ball player thanks mother, God, truth, justice and the American way of life.

Early Wynn is not inclined toward sentimentality. He had won three hundred games, working through four decades in the major leagues, and he had intimidated generations of American League batters with the best knockdown pitching of his time. He deserved to be in the Hall of Fame, he knew. He pulled the cork from a bottle of Seagram's Crown Royal. He took a drink.

The telephone rang. It was an enthusiastic young man from a wire service. "Hall of Fame?" Early Wynn thought. "It's a Hall of Shame. I should have been voted in three years ago." But Mr. Wynn can drink heartily without losing either his footing or his senses. He buried his impulse and made a measured response. "Naturally I'm happy. I don't think I'm as thrilled as I would have been if I had made it the first time. I'd like to have been with Stan Musial, Ted Williams, Walter Johnson. They all made it the first year they were eligible."

The following summer Wynn went to work managing Orlando, the Minnesota farm team in the Class A Florida State League. It pleased him to manage in the Minnesota organization under Calvin Griffith because Calvin's father, Clark Griffith, had brought Wynn into the majors in 1939. He took a few days off for induction ceremonies at Cooperstown that August and did make sentimental comments in a speech. That may have been an error. Cal Griffith fired him from Orlando in September, making Wynn the only man I know who was trumpeted into the Hall of Fame and booted out of organized baseball in successive months.

The business of baseball offers a full quota of absurdities. In the low minors, where ball players are supposed to be learning, you find one man, the manager, charged with teaching twenty-three different apprentices. In the majors, where ball players are supposed to be finished, you find special coaches for pitching, catching and even base running. The big leagues have expanded chaotically, and clubs that might have become intense and profitable rivals, say Oakland and San Francisco, play in different leagues. It is tempting, then, to regard Wynn's dismissal as one more instance of thoughtlessness on baseball's windy heights. Some, knowing the Minnesota organization, suggest that Griffith simply wanted to find someone else who would manage for $500 less. I suspect other considerations were involved.

Wynn is a fierce, direct man who can take a drink. Don Newcombe could take a drink, too, and Newcombe told a Senate subcommittee in March, 1976, that whiskey had cost him everything but his life.

Alcohol has threatened baseball players from the beginning of the professional game. By layman's standards, a ball player works a short day. He has more idle hours than most in which to raise a glass. A ball player does not have to reach an office by 9 A.M. After a drinking night, he has all morning to recover. A ball player travels. In adolescent fantasy, the road is a roseland of dancing girls, some topless, all beckoning. The road is free. Actual baseball travel quickly becomes a monotony of stations and airports, buses and room clerks—in short, homelessness. For every night when a dancing girl beckons, if that is what one wants, there are five in which a man aches to see his wife, his children, even his backyard. Certain ball players drink to forget their loneliness and keep drinking until they can no longer remember what they had started drinking to forget.

A Penobscot Indian from Maine named Louis Francis Sockalexis batted .331 for Cleveland as a rookie in 1897. He could run a hundred yards in ten seconds, while in full baseball uniform, and is said to have possessed the best throwing arm of his time. He started drinking on the road and, in a wretched enactment of the Indian-firewater cliché, Lou Sockalexis destroyed himself. He dropped out of the majors in three years and, according to the historian Robert Smith, "became a street beggar, shuffling along sidewalks, with the toes out of his shoes, and his hand extended for the few cents he needed to get a mouthful of whiskey."

Ed Delahanty came out of a Cleveland family that produced five boys who made the major leagues. Ed was the best. In 1893, when the standard baseball was as lively as a roll of socks, Delahanty hit nineteen home runs. He made money and began to worry about keeping it. His wife liked parties. He worried about her fidelity. Drunk, he could forget why he was worrying.

He had been drinking hard on a train in the summer of 1903, when he decided to go for a walk during a layover at the Niagara Falls station. He chose a railroad bridge as his footpath, lost his balance and fell into the Niagara River, boiling below. The day he died, Big Ed Delahanty was batting .333.

Baseball literature bubbles with drinking stories, usually told in macho-romantic style and ending with a snappy punch line. "So when I asked Paul Waner how he could hit when he was smashed, Waner said, 'I see three baseballs, but I only swing at the middle one.'" The late John Lardner once picked his all-time, all-alcoholic All-Stars. It was a funny idea and a championship team. The right-fielder was Babe Ruth.

But alcoholism was humorless to Don Newcombe. "Mr. Chairman," he began at a Senate hearing, "my drinking started when I was eight. When I joined the Dodgers, my consumption increased tremendously. Baseball managers encouraged drinking beer. They still do. The only way to celebrate a victory is to knock off a six-pack. When Mickey Mantle and Whitey Ford brag in a TV commercial that they belong in the beer drinkers' Hall of Fame, they're not kidding.

"My problem was that I never knew my capacity. After my biggest season with the Dodgers—in 1956 I won twenty-seven games—I went to Japan with the team. I was so constantly drunk I couldn't pitch a single game. The following year I went into a prolonged slump. I dropped back into the minor leagues.

"My personal life fell apart. I was divorced from my first wife. I lost my career in baseball. Then I lost a cocktail lounge, a liquor store and an apartment house—all my investments. I went bankrupt and lost the family home.

"One day my second wife told me she'd had enough." Newcombe paused and gazed at the politicians around him. "Gentlemen, I would give anything under the sun not to lose my wife. I promised her on the head of my oldest son that I wouldn't drink again. I haven't since 1966."

The difference between Newcombe and Early Wynn defines the borderline between drinking and alcoholism. Wynn could mix hard stuff with wine, across a convivial evening, and run at eleven the next morning. Then with hard stuff of another sort, he'd pitch a shutout.

I heard a baseball writer mention once that Early couldn't manage well in the major leagues because he drank.

"Write that," I said, "and you'll be sued for libel."

"Don't you know him?" the writer said. "Haven't you gone drinking with him?"

"For twenty years and I've never seen him drunk."

To Wynn, convivial gatherings were a delight of big league life. He went to parties and he gave parties, gay raucous evenings, rich in baseball talk and needling, and, with a single exception, he did not overestimate his capacity. On that one careless night he was working for Cleveland and visiting Bill Veeck, who owned the Indians. Martinis preceded dinner. Stingers followed. "Curiously, I don't remember exactly what we served next," Veeck says, "but I do recall that at 4:30 in the morning I was mixing grasshoppers. Then it struck Early. He was scheduled to pitch the next day and here he was drinking late with the boss."

"I better go home," Wynn said. "One-o'clock game."

"It's too late to worry about sleep now," Veeck said. "You better just keep going."

Wynn reached the ball park at eleven, put on a rubber jacket and began to run. He sweated and showered and went out and pitched a shutout. "Then the reporters came," Veeck says, "and Early answered all their questions. He got somebody with the knuckle ball. Someone else was fooled by a high slider. He did just fine until the last reporter left the dressing room. Then he fell over on his face."

There was nothing bland about Early, nothing subdued, nothing cautious. He didn't like hitters and he said he didn't like hitters. He knocked them down.

"Why should I worry about hitters?" Wynn said. "Do they worry about me? Do you ever find a hitter crying because he's hit a line drive through the box? My job is getting hitters out. If I don't get them out, I lose. I don't like losing a ball game any more than a salesman likes losing a sale. I've got a right to knock down anybody holding a bat."

"Suppose it was your own mother?" a reporter said.

Wynn thought briefly. "Mother was a pretty good curve-ball hitter," he said.

That was humor, but at Yankee Stadium I saw Wynn brush his own son. Joe Early, a tall, rangy boy, was visiting for a day, and Early volunteered to throw a little batting practice. Joe Early hit a long line drive to left center. The next pitch, at the cheekbone, sent Joe Early diving to the ground.

"You shouldn't crowd me," Wynn said, with noncommittal tenderness.

He taught himself rope tricks and played supermarket openings. He began a newspaper column and within a month had attacked general managers for their penury and the *Sporting News* for publishing too much gossip. Flying bothered him, so he took lessons and bought himself a single-engine plane. (It still bothered him to ride as a passenger.) He acquired a cabin cruiser and a motorbike and a Packard and a Mercedes, leading Shirley Povich of the Washington *Post* to comment, "Early does not lack for transportation." Wynn seized life with his great hands, implacably determined to wring every syllable of living from his time.

Despite that intensity, his staying power was prodigious. He pitched for the Senators in 1939, moved on to the great Indian staff, with Bob Feller and Bob Lemon in 1949, and, ten years after *that,* pitched the Chicago

White Sox to a pennant and won the Cy Young award. He was a thick-chested, black-haired man with a natural glower, which he directed at batters like a death ray. He seemed eternal. But in the early 1960s, he began to suffer attacks of gout. On a snap throw to first, he strained muscles near his elbow and the gout moved into his pitching arm. It was time to quit, but he wanted to win his three hundredth.

His legs were weakening. "During those last years," Lorraine Wynn says, "when he'd come back from running, his legs would be so sore we had to work out this routine. He'd lie down on his stomach and I'd take a rolling pin and move it up and down over the backs of his legs. That was the only thing that seemed to relax the muscles."

The old fast ball was gone. It took him three years to win his final sixteen games, and it would not be until 1963 that he won his three hundredth. He had to pitch in pain and terrible weariness, but three hundred was the goal and he was going to get there. "Hell, I've lost more than two hundred," he said.

His rage to live persisted and one night he asked if there were any interesting parties in New York. We tried one, which was dull, and another, which was worse. "Let's go to the Village Barn," he said.

"That's way downtown," I said, "and I haven't been there since college."

"I just want to see that place one more time."

The Barn was barren. It was getting very late. We took some drinks.

"The hitters may not know this," Wynn said. "They aren't all that smart. But I know it. I can't get 'em out any more."

"You're in your forties, Early. What did you figure? You knew this was going to happen."

His face assumed a look of inexpressible sadness. "But now it's *happening,*" he said.

After retiring, he drifted through a predictable mix of baseball jobs: pitching coach, scout, minor league manager. But he never became a politic man. In 1969, when Billy Martin managed the Twins, one columnist's story enraged Martin. Three sportswriters, Red Smith among them, appeared on the field. Martin began cursing at the perfidy of the press. "Anyone who talks to any of those newspaper bastards is crazy," Martin yelled.

Wynn had known Smith for fifteen years. He was also Martin's pitching coach. Before Billy Martin's popping eyes, Wynn walked over to Smith and welcomed him warmly to the field. He was not Martin's pitching coach again.

I spent a week with Wynn in Orlando during 1972, riding buses through central Florida, working out with the team when he'd let me, tasting life at the bottom of the minor leagues. He seemed to be an excellent manager. Some of the players, notably pitchers, were awed, so Early took them to dinner or visited their homes. To me he said, "I sort of have to be head counselor." The Twins resisted the idea of supplying beer for the team bus. Early bought the beer out of his own pocket.

His pitching approach is unusual in that he believes in

the high slider. Usually you throw the fast ball up and the slider down. Wynn explained how to use the slider high. "Start with a bad one, that breaks wide. Bad pitch, but till it breaks it looks okay. He goes for it and misses and you have your strike. Try with something else, the curve, or for me the knuckler, and you can get a second strike. Now throw a spinner—not a slider but a ball that spins and looks like it's gonna slide—just where you threw that first pitch. He thinks it will break wide again. He doesn't swing, and you've got called strike three. Of course, you've got to put something on the ball."

He meant throw hard, but few of the Orlando pitchers were really fast. The team went nowhere and Griffith forced Wynn out of baseball.

Early handled a bat well enough to pinch-hit for Washington. He was a switch hitter who once batted .319. He was a scholar of the game, and whenever I've watched him teach, he's been both stern and patient. The knockdown pitch has been curtailed by a change in the rules, but I don't think that's why nobody has hired Wynn.

Baseball executives increasingly favor men who are corporate bland. More and more major league teams are run by syndicates, and syndicates prefer managers and coaches who do as they are told, salute the company president and study statistics rather than spend spirited evenings talking baseball with the press. Veeck might have brought him to Chicago, but Paul Richards wanted to be his own pitching coach. Finley? Proud, independent field leaders are not to Charley Finley's taste.

With few exceptions, managers today are organization

men, who sip coffee and a few beers, praise their superiors, play golf, exude conventionalism. Wynn is an unconventional man, up from the Great Depression, with a record of saying what he thinks, a love of frank talk toward the dawn, a distaste for defeat and an absolute intolerance of anything less than an ultimate effort every game. Who in baseball today would hire a manager like that? The question answers itself pragmatically. Nobody.

Wynn has found work as sales coordinator for Wellcraft, a successful boat-manufacturing company, and flying south I expected to find him depressed, or at least subdued.

He lives in Nokomis, forty minutes south of the Wellcraft assembly plant in Sarasota. The Hall of Fame pitcher commutes to his office every morning. "The traffic," he said, the old rage still intact. "What the hell do government officials think about, if they do think? What the hell do they think the west coast of Florida is, a slum? It was no secret that more and more people would be moving here. We knew it twenty years ago. Why haven't they put in first-class roads?"

We wandered outside his house, which I first visited in 1954. It stood in the country then. Today other houses crowd close. He started his boat and we headed toward an inland waterway, once a blue corridor of beauty. There were little mangrove islands then, and channel markers. A pelican sat on each marker. As the boat approached, the pelican suddenly flew off. Later we fished in the Gulf of Mexico and I caught a can of Budweiser.

Now the inland waterway runs between huge condominiums with white concrete sundecks and yellow shuffleboard courts. "I didn't used to know what ecology meant," Wynn said as we cruised. "I sure as hell do now. I guess while I was up there pitching, somebody forgot to put in zoning laws."

We turned around and docked and walked into his party room. The bar was supported by bats. Overhead, baseballs from fifteen of his greatest victories hung from the ceiling. He had placed his Cy Young trophy on one wall. From another, three men smiled out of an old picture: Stan Musial, Ted Williams, Early Wynn.

"The Hall of Fame," I began.

"Look," he said, "you know I'm honored to be in there. Hartford, Alabama, that's where I grew, and the biggest thing that happened in that town was a peanut festival. But we had baseball and we'd ride mule wagons many a mile for a town game. They write when I showed up at a pro tryout I was barefoot. I wasn't, but I was wearing overalls. It's a long way from Hartford, Alabama, to Cooperstown, but I mean, hell, any man who wins three hundred major league games ought to get voted in as soon as he's eligible. I mean, don't people know how much hard work that is?"

I said I thought I did and asked how he liked the job at Wellcraft. "Well, I've always been fond of boats," he said. He took out a catalogue and then, the fiercest competitor I've known in baseball, set about selling me a cabin cruiser.

A light checking account blocked the sale, but this wasn't precisely like a Wynn ball game. Among the trophies and the photographs I knew at last I could resist his will, without getting a fast ball fired at my head.

Walter O'Malley, in his windowed office at Dodger Stadium. Cigar is poised for thrust.

O'Malley Stadium (and gold mine) on a typical Sunday afternoon.

Indoor baseball: The Astros playing at the Dome in an unusual circumstance. Stands are full.

(Wendy Kahn)

Wally Moon managing at John Brown University, not from the bench but from a chair.

(Photo by the author)

John Felske, manager of the Berkshire Brewers, warming up before a game against the Waterbury, Connecticut, Dodgers in 1976. Neither Berkshire nor Waterbury survived as Eastern League franchises in 1977.

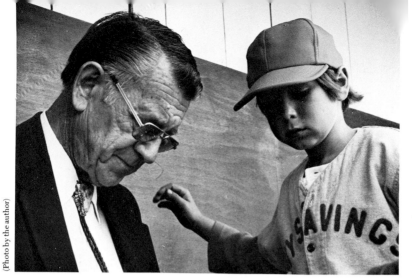

(Photo by the author)

Lefty Gomez signs an autograph for a Little Leaguer.

(Photo by the author)

Students from Williams and Amherst and a top-hatted umpire, before a replay of a nineteenth-century ball game.

(Brian Lawker for *Sports Illustrated.* © Time, Inc.)

Artie Wilson, a superstar with the Birmingham Black Barons, reached his prime when the majors were closed to blacks. He now sells cars in Oregon.

(Wendy Kahn)

Stan Musial smiling as he remembers battering Dodger pitching years ago.

(Barney Stein)

Hall of Fame pitcher Early Wynn, under a portrait of Christy Mathewson.

(Photo by the author)

Sculptor Juan Orcera at work on clay model of a statue of
Roberto Clemente, later to be cast in bronze. Clay model of
Little Leaguer stands in foreground.

Bill Veeck of the White Sox sits against his usual 1976 backdrop: empty seats.

Business Manager Rudie Schaffer on drums, Field Manager Paul Richards with flag, and Bill Veeck on fife offer a Bicentennial moment at Comiskey Park in 1976. This was opening day. The White Sox went downhill thereafter.

(Wide World Photos)

George Foster and Cesar Geronimo greet Bench at the plate after one of his home runs in the 1976 Series. Rival catcher Thurman Munson seems to miss the spirit of the moment.

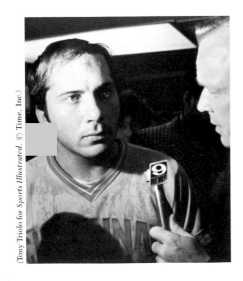

(Tony Triolo for *Sports Illustrated.* © Time, Inc.)

Johnny Bench, intense in a personal and team triumph, hears out a reporter after the 1976 World Series.

(Photo by the author)

Roger Laurence Kahn, retired Little League baseball player, spending a season on the ice.

5

The Children of Roberto

On a flat Puerto Rican plain, beside Avenida Iturregui and a pleasant subdivision called Country Club, four hundred barren acres stretched under a pitiless sun. Part of the land lay dry and caked; part still was marsh. This was Ciudad Deportiva, Sports City, the last dream Roberto Clemente voiced before a DC-7, overloaded and under-manned, carried him to death in the Caribbean Sea on the rainy night of December 31, 1972. He had lined his three thousandth major league hit, a double riding deep into left center field, three months before. He was thirty-eight years old.

I suppose sociologists would find Clemente's dream naïve. He wanted to build a Puerto Rican sports camp, free to all but open only to the very poor, so that, as he said, "every single child from poverty can learn to play sports and maybe make some success as I did." By now

more than $800,000 had been collected for Ciudad
Deportiva and three and a half years had passed since
Clemente's death. On the barren plain two bulldozers
worked at a languorous pace inimical to Roberto Clemente.

Certain rumors persist about the death of Clemente,
neither a saint nor a tramp, only a gifted ball player with
a social conscience. "Bobby had a broad in Nicaragua,"
someone insists. "That's the real reason he took that
flight." Another Puerto Rican suggests that the plane con-
tained gold, or U.S. dollars, which Clemente was going to
sequester beyond the grasp of tax authorities.

These are the facts. During November of 1972 Clemente had taken an amateur Puerto Rican baseball team
to play a series of games in Nicaragua. He had liked riding
in oxcarts as a boy in Carolina, his home village, and in
Nicaragua he saw oxcarts again. He also met a hospital-
ized child without legs. He asked why the child had no
artificial legs.

"We don't have any money," the boy said, in Spanish.
"Legs would cost $800."

"When I go back to Puerto Rico, I will raise the money,"
Clemente promised.

Five weeks later Managua was flattened by six violent
shocks. Howard Hughes flew away at the first tremor. In
Puerto Rico Clemente organized a relief campaign. He
appeared on television and radio, pleading for money,
morphine, sugar. Although his back ached, he helped load
supplies on trucks in a staging area near Hiram Bithorn
Stadium. Then word reached him that soldiers in the

Nicaraguan Army were stealing the supplies and selling sugar to people who were starving, and morphine to people who writhed in agony.

Clemente remembered the oxcarts and the crippled boy. He was the finest of Latin ball players and he had a strong sense of his own fame. "If I go to Nicaragua, the stealing will stop," he said, beating a palm against his iron chest. "They would not steal from Roberto Clemente."

A palm on his chest was Clemente's way of displaying earnest pride. His career, he liked to say, was proof "the Latin ball player is no hot dog." The Dodger organization let him go to Pittsburgh in 1955 for a confusion of motives. What troubled Clemente was his suspicion of a quota system. The Dodger roster was already heavy with black ball players. "And me," he would say, "I am a double nigger. I am a nigger because I am black and a nigger because I am Puertorriqueño."

In 1971, when the Pirates defeated Baltimore in an exciting World Series, Clemente batted .414 and hit a home run in the sixth game and the seventh. He was chosen Most Valuable Player by *Sport Magazine*. With the honor comes a luncheon and a free car. For the honor, a man must make a speech.

A politician from San Juan introduced Clemente. He was a puffy, rotund man and whiskey had made him prolix and maundering. The audience sat in boredom and embarrassment. But when Clemente rose, it was as if he had been introduced by Demosthenes.

"I am thirty-seven years old," he began, "and I was a poor boy in the village of Carolina and I have always

played hard and run out every hit and this is the first time
I have ever been asked to speak in New York City." Hearing him, one listened to an overflowing heart.

"I've been to a lot of these luncheons," I told him afterward, "and that was the best speech I've heard."

Clemente did not smile. The palm beat on the left side
of his chest. "From here," he said. "It was good and true
because it came from here."

After the earthquake that next year, a jet was available
to ferry supplies from San Juan to Managua. The DC-7
would be cheaper, leaving more money to purchase
medicines. During Christmas week, the DC-7 crashed
into a cyclone fence after its brakes failed. Clemente said
he did not care. "The brakes can be fixed."

A DC-7 is a big, four-engine turboprop plane, usually
flown by a trained crew of three. The pilot, a man named
Hill, was fully licensed. The co-pilot, Arthur Rivera,
owned the aircraft, but he did not have a valid certificate
to act as first officer, a fact he never revealed to Clemente.
Instead, he said, "Would I myself take off if anything were
wrong? Above all people, I value myself most."

The third seat in the cockpit properly is occupied by a
flight engineer. Arthur Rivera could not find an engineer
willing to work on New Year's Eve. He hired an aircraft
mechanic. The plane was loaded in haste until its gross
take-off weight totaled 4,193 pounds more than the maxi-
mum allowed by the Federal Aviation Authority. At least
sixteen sixty-pound sacks of sugar were piled behind the
cockpit. According to Cristóbal Colón, who accompanied
Clemente to the plane, the sugar sacks were not lashed
down.

As the plane accelerated down the runway at 9:20 P.M., one engine began to sputter. A flight engineer, studying the analyzers that show the condition of each engine, can make an instant diagnosis. If necessary, he shouts, "Abort, abort." A mechanic lacks the training and the experience to make such a decision.

The plane took off. Another engine coughed. On the tape of the plane's transmission to the tower you can hear the pilot say, without panic, "This is NC 500, comin' back around." The pilot banked steeply. Perhaps the bags of sugar shifted. In the blackness of a winter rainstorm, NC 500 continued to bank and slipped sideways into twelve-foot waves at approximately 150 miles an hour. The aircraft might as well have flown into a wall of concrete.

"It was so sad for all of us," said Luis Rodriguez Mayoral, a Pittsburgh Pirate scout who guided me about his island. "In one year we lost two great heroes. Roberto and Don Pablo Casals. But do people remember? If they did, wouldn't Ciudad Deportiva be more than this by now?" He gestured toward the plain, simmering in a tropic summer.

Latins have a gift for patient melancholy, but Mayoral brightened quickly. "I will show you, *amigo,* that there is nothing else sad about baseball on our island. Our island baseball is wonderful, *tu sabe?*"

Puerto Rican baseball is a joyous pastime, played mostly for the wonder of the game. Stateside one hears that Puerto Ricans play ball because anything, even catching a double-header in July, is preferable to cutting sugar in the canebrakes. That was true in Clemente's boyhood when, as he liked to recount, he earned a few pennies a

day carrying jugs of milk to sweltering field hands. But
Puerto Rico has become a relatively prosperous island.
Attracted by tolerant tax laws, American electronics firms
(GTE-Sylvania) and cosmetic companies (Avon Products)
have moved factories there. Beyond rum and tourism, the
island boasts scores of varied industries. Most willing
workers can find jobs. Puerto Ricans play baseball now
because they love the game. It is their national fanaticism.

The island's seventy-six towns and barrios are organized into an endless summer of baseball. Boys from four
to eight are grouped into a category called Piruli. They
play with plastic balls and bats. Then, those with ability
move successively to Little Leagues, Boys' Baseball and
Babe Ruth Leagues. After that, as in the continental
United States, the best athletes sign with scouts like Mayoral. Boys of good but lesser skills remain. Many play amateur baseball until their thirties.

The season of the Puerto Rican Central Amateur
League lasts from July to January. The Puerto Rican Amateur Federation begins its schedule in February and runs
through autumn. Unlike the continental United States,
every Puerto Rican town has its team, peopled by local
semi-pros. Like Mayoral, most dreamed of being Clemente. But when the dream failed, they kept on playing.
Town ball, not sugar cane, covers the island. For nine
months a year Puerto Rico glows with lights shining on a
hundred baseball fields.

Mounting Mayoral's Volkswagen Beetle, we bounced
about San Juan, and the village called Guaynabo and into
Caguas, a small city settled under hills along a road lined

by flamboyants, a tree blossoming with rust-red flowers. We watched Little League ball in Carolina, now a suburb in the San Juan sprawl, and we saw amateurs play in Las Piedras, The Rocks, a town so small that it does not appear on tourist maps, and where the single saloon is called, for reasons nobody knows, the Guadalcanal Bar.

"We have a problem," Vic Power, the old major league first baseman, said as he studied fourteen-year-olds on a cloudy day at a dusty little field in Caguas. "We have much participation. *Too* much participation. *Too* many dreams of the major leagues. I see a good ball player. I have to tell him, it is ten thousand to one he will not make the major leagues. Sometimes I have to tell them it is one hundred thousand to one, because if you are both black and Puertorriqueño, they will not easily accept you. It will be very much more difficult."

Power's memories of playing as a black are cold and somewhat bitter, an opposite of the genial recollections you find in Artie Wilson.

"It was very bad when I got to the States," Power said. "I am strong and not afraid, but I do not want to be murdered and when I first came to Florida for training in Fort Myers, I was afraid to cross the street. One night, three white men stood on the other side. I could see from the way they held themselves that it would be bad if we came close together.

"The light was green. They walked across the street. I stood in a doorway, and as you see I am very black. I hoped they would not notice me. They did not. They passed. When the light was red, I went across the street.

"The policeman came from nowhere. He held my shoulder and he had a gun and he said I was arrested for crossing against the light. He took me to court and the judge looked at me in a hard way and this is what I said:

" 'I am Puertorriqueño and a ball player and I do not know how it is in the continental States. I thought the green light meant for whites to cross and the red light meant black people could cross the street.' "

"What did the judge tell you?" I asked Power.

"He said he didn't believe me and the case was dismissed and that I should never again appear before him in court."

Power told harder stories then, mostly sexual and bellicose. But Ted Williams liked him, and he was proud of that. When Jimmy Piersall called him a black bastard, Power recognized Piersall's intensity and his own strength and withdrew. And Early Wynn, oh Early Wynn. He lived in Florida, where the police had been cruel to blacks, but he was a very good pitcher.

You watch the shortstop. When you are looking at a team you have not seen before, watch the shortstop, who must move laterally and charge slow twisting ground balls and make the play. Neither fourteen-year-old shortstop before Power and myself looked promising to me. Vic Power agreed. We were not seeing the best of Puerto Rican ball games. "In New York," he said, "in what you call Spanish Harlem, do they still remember the Gold Gloves I won for fielding?"

The baseball cast is always changing, and in Spanish Harlem now, people talk of Felix Millan and John Cande-

laria and Willie Montanez. "Sure they remember your
Gold Gloves," I told Power.

He beamed. "This one team," he said, "is called Café
Crema, after a big coffee company which gives them uniforms. It is not the best team and Café Crema is not the
best coffee. When you have lunch, order our other coffee,
Café Rico."

Mayoral drove me to the development called Country
Club for a Little League play-off. At Parque Angel Ramos,
a manicured field set among tidy suburban homes, two
hundred people cheered and watched and listened to
Carlos de Jesus broadcast over loudspeakers. Country
Club defeated Valle Ariba, 9 to 0, and the Country Club
shortstop, Jorge Burgos, played impressively.

In the fifth inning, with the Country Club's victory already safe, a Valle Ariba base runner reached second. The
next pitch bounded five feet from the catcher. The runner did not try to advance, but when I looked up, there
was shortstop Jorge Burgos backing up third.

"Good play," I told the twelve-year-old after the game.

"Not a good play," he corrected me in Spanish. "Just the
play you're supposed to make." His face was long and
bronze and free of lines.

"Would you like to be a major leaguer?"

"In my short life," Jorge Burgos said, "I have accomplished little aside from baseball. So my answer is, yes, I
would like to play there. But perhaps later, when I accom-
plish other things, my answer would be different."

When Guaynabo played Cayey, two town teams meeting at the modern ball park at Guaynabo, two thousand

fans showed up at 9:45 Saturday morning. Guaynabo's uniforms were blue and white. Cayey wore orange. The game stayed close. The visiting Guaynabo squad was leading by two runs. Then a cloudburst struck. The home team's ground crew moved so slowly that the field was drenched. The fans chattered and applauded and sipped beer. A drunk began to curse and wave his arms. Four children started a game of punchball, using a crushed paper cup as their *pelota*. The drunk shouted at the children. A policeman grabbed him from behind and shoved him toward a gate and out of the park. The Cayey manager announced that he was protesting the game "because of Guaynabo's lazy ground crew." The people of Guaynabo hooted and laughed. "If we were ahead at Cayey and it rained," a man said to me in Spanish, "would not their ground crew be even lazier than ours?"

"Cayey is a pretty town," Mayoral said, "among mountains and not far from lakes."

The downpour continued. The fans sat chattering. The ball park was their town meeting hall. When the game was called, two hours later, and everyone went home, they were still chattering in good cheer.

Near a barren field in Las Piedras, on the narrow road that twists toward Humacao Beach, a young man was playing pepper with his son. Their names were José Soto, Junior and Senior, and after Mayoral introduced us, Mr. Soto said, "Vic Power tells me my child's swing is so good I should not touch it."

"*¿Tu eres de Nueva York?*" the boy asked. Was I from New York?

"Yes."

Had I seen the Yankees? Would I watch him?

The father gabbled like a salesman, and José Soto who was seven swung wildly and then missed six ground balls out of eight.

"He moves well," I told the father.

"If you come back to Las Piedras," Mr. Soto said, "understand you always will be welcome."

That night I attended a Bicentennial banquet at the Caribe Hilton sponsored by the Association of the U.S. Army. The room was thick with braid and brass and the menu included such dishes as Yankee Pot Roast, Revere Cheese Pie and Liberty Tomato. The guest of honor was an astronaut and Marine officer named Jack Robert Lousma, who piloted Skylab 2 and said he had logged fourteen hundred hours in space.

Colonel Lousma presented the Governor of Puerto Rico with a photo of San Juan taken from a height of 270 miles. Then he made a curious speech. It was strange and beautiful in space, Lousma said, and one thing he'd noticed was that you could not see the boundary lines between countries. Nevertheless, none of us should forget the constant peril of Godless atheistic Communism. The military men, some Puerto Rican but mostly continental Americans, cheered. "Our space technology," Lousma said, "benefits every single person on this island." The band played "Dixie." A hundred officers sprang to attention.

I don't think José Soto, Jr. would have been able to make any more sense than I out of Lousma's speech.

Puerto Rico is not poor compared to Haiti, but the median income is $2,328 per person. In the barrios, the billions we invest in space appear irrelevant.

But baseball came to Puerto Rico in 1900, introduced by occupation soldiers after the Spanish-American War. That is the single continental export almost every islander understands and watches and plays.

"My friend," Mayoral said at the airport, "what you should help continental Americans understand is not only that we love baseball but that we are good players and we are proud that we are good. We are a tiny island and some of our politics is crazy, but you know how all of us want to feel? Before he died, flying into the rain, Roberto Clemente said, 'I would like to be remembered as a ball player who gave all he had to give.' That is it. The opposite of lazy. Our dedication. ¿Tu sabe?"

I said I thought I did.

6

William the Unconquerable

Sometime, somewhere, there will be a club nobody really wants. And then Ole Will will come
wandering along to laugh some more.
Look for me under the arc lights, boys. I'll be
back.
—BILL VEECK, 1962

It had been a long time between ball clubs, and Bill Veeck
was right. The Chicago White Sox were a club that defied
you to want them. The pitching was uncertain. The
catcher was embarrassing. The outfielders shared one
weakness to a man. They were not very good at catching
fly balls.

In mid-September, a raucous convention of machinery
salesmen crowded Chicago hotels with burly men from
Wyoming, Indiana, Washington State. Perhaps fifty of
them stood in the lobby of the Lake Shore Holiday Inn,
waiting for rooms and showers at seven o'clock on a warm
and humid night. Some grumbled. Others raised their
voices. A wispish, patient, frightened room clerk said over
and over, "We're going to straighten things out. The computer has broken down. Sorry. It's not my fault. I can't
help it. The computer."

The grumbling men were cramped hip to hip in the narrow lobby. I thought some might wander off toward Bill Veeck's ball park for his twilight double-header. I hoped so. The season was winding down and the White Sox clutched last place as though it were a 24-carat ring.

Drunks spilled from the hotel bar, clapping each other on the back.

"Hey, you old bastard. I saw ya pat the dolly's ass."

"That was warm-up time. Let's start the game."

"Damn right, Chuck. Where're the broads?"

There were not enough women, either amateur or professional, to go round. Overcrowded Chicago was short of everything but noise.

My taxi inched through traffic toward the Dan Ryan Expressway, which leads south toward Thirty-fifth Street and Comiskey Park, a pleasant double-decked stadium that was opened on July 1, 1910. During the 1950s, when Veeck first ran the White Sox, he installed high-intensity lights in adjoining streets. South Chicago was beginning to spawn muggers. He preserved the old trees that rise on Shields Avenue. He had whitewash applied to the outside concrete walls. He repainted the seats. The ball park was at once venerable and contemporary. It was a clean, well-lighted place to see a game.

This night the White Sox were playing the Kansas City Royals. By now the mighty Reds had outdistanced the Dodgers. The Phillies had ground a winning edge; they would beat Pittsburgh. Smart trades and syndicate cash had vitalized the Yankees; they would bring a pennant flag to the South Bronx. The race between first-place Kansas City and Oakland in the Western Division of the American League seemed the only one truly in doubt. Veeck's double-header bore on that race. It was an interesting attraction.

Comiskey Park was still the clean, well-lighted place that I remembered. Concessions beckoned with awnings of bright stripes. The walls were loud with baseball posters, painted by schoolchildren, for a competition Veeck underwrote with a $1,000 prize. I rode an elevator to the roof and then proceeded on a wooden catwalk toward an old iron door into the press box. Before me, real grass stretched toward the center-field fence, 415 feet away from home plate. There a scoreboard rose above the stands. Inside, a fireworks specialist stood beside his wares. At the first White Sox home run, he would light the sky with rockets.

It was a typical Bill Veeck ball park, combining comfort, tradition and sideshows, except for the crowd. There wasn't any. About 5,000 customers sat scattered among 45,000 seats. Put differently, 40,000 empty seats spread wide between clumps of fans. The machinery salesmen, like most of America, were ignoring the return of William Veeck.

He sat in the press box, wearing old slacks and a sports shirt, studying journeymen named Bannister, Johnson and Orta. He sees things quickly, like a good field manager. He smokes constantly. The more serious he is, the more softly he speaks. While a young pitcher named Chris Knapp threw hard, protecting Chicago's one-run lead, I asked about the banks of unsold seats.

"People misinterpret," Veeck said, very quietly. "I've never suggested that promotions do much if you aren't winning. That isn't the psychology of the fan. The fans identify with the home team. When the home team wins, they feel that they win, too. They get away from the galling losses of life. When the home team gets beat, the way we've been getting beaten this season, you get negative identification. The White Sox lose and the White Sox fans feel they lose with us. At the ball park, they get the same rich fulfilling experience they get when they're three months late in payments to the Friendly Finance Company." Veeck coughed and lit a cigarette. "What I do say is promotions plus a winning team will break attendance. That's what happened when we had winners in here and in Cleveland and in Milwaukee a long time ago."

He puffed. "Did I ever tell you I wanted to sign a black in Milwaukee about 1940, six years before they signed Jackie Robinson?"

"Why didn't you?"

"Because the Commissioner, Kenesaw Mountain Landis, said if I tried it, I'd be thrown out of baseball for life."

In 1943, far from his customary playgrounds, Veeck served as a Marine private on a small Pacific island called Bougainville. He was thirty years old, and already renowned. He could have been an officer, but braid and Bill Veeck are inimical.

Someone prematurely fired an artillery piece toward unseen battalions of Japanese infantrymen. The cannon recoiled into Veeck's right foot, and cut a ragged gash to the bone. The wound was patched and Veeck rejoined his platoon. A few months later the foot was badly swollen. What he describes as "jungle rot" was attacking the bone that had been bared.

Surgery by Marine physicians proved inadequate. The jungle rot moved slowly toward his shin. In 1946, civilian doctors amputated the lower portion of the leg, but like the Marine doctors, they miscalculated. They cut too low. Soon Veeck needed a second amputation. Such maiming surgery continued for a decade. Something always went wrong. Full of good intentions, some doctor always made a mistake. At length, Veeck had to undergo thirty-one surgical procedures. Finally, nothing was left but a stump, barely long enough to support a prosthetic device. He has born his mutilation with less complaint than you hear from people who have had a tooth extracted under anesthesia.

"Does this team and these empty seats bother you?" I said in the press box.

"We'll be all right. We can be all right. But I want to have a winner in three years. That's an unchanging formula of baseball. Give them a winner in three years, or else you'll turn your fans off for a decade." Another cigarette. "We're reasonably capitalized, but we aren't here to spend a decade of defeat."

"Your health?"

"Well, of course, I can't see as well as I could and I have to wear glasses. Watching this team, nonvision eases the pain. My hearing was dulled permanently when that artillery piece went off in Bougainville, but I'm used to that by now. What does bother me is my left leg, my only leg.

There's some kind of arthritis that's developed in the knee. I don't believe in owners' boxes. I sit with the fans or with the writers. I was sitting out in center with some customers one day this summer and I started back toward the press box and I got stuck. With the arthritis and the artificial leg, I simply couldn't get any farther. I was marooned in my own ball park. That was embarrassing.

"I've lost good knee action in my leg. American technicians have developed an artificial joint that's fine for going slowly. The Russians have developed one that lets you move. But Health, Education and Welfare has gotten very careful about the work of foreign doctors. They remember Thalidomide. I don't want an old man's knee, so I have to wait for the government to approve the Russian device before I'll let them do an implant. Meanwhile, I've had to give up tennis."

I looked at him. Bespectacled, grizzled, running a last-place team that couldn't even draw bored traveling salesmen with expense accounts. Poor by contrast to the men who own the Dodgers, Reds and Yankees. Somewhat deaf, missing one leg and suffering from arthritis in the other. At sixty-three, his one complaint was that he missed his tennis. I can think of no better definition of indomitable.

I caught his style in 1959, when Early Wynn pitched an elderly White Sox ball club to a pennant. That was the season in which Wally Moon's home runs won the pennant for the patchwork L.A. Dodgers. The World Series did not exalt baseball as an art form. But Comiskey Park sold out quickly, and the Dodgers, playing in the Coliseum, sold ninety thousand tickets for each of the three middle games.

Amid all this cash flow, Walter O'Malley decided to close the Dodger hospitality room at 10 P.M. A World Series hospitality room offers baseball writers, managers, coaches, pretty much everyone of consequence except the competing athletes, a chance to eat and drink without charge. The room is both a source of news, particularly as liquor loosens tongues, and a way that underpaid newspapermen can bill their papers for meals and drinks they have never bought. In 1959, the phrase "underpaid newspaperman" was a tautology. Accepting rotten wages was a condition of employment. Knowing this, O'Malley closed his drinking room at ten. Ah, penury is made of most stern stuff.

Responding, Veeck announced, "When we get back to Chicago, gentlemen, our hospitality room will be open twenty-four hours a day. You are welcome to have Scotch with breakfast or for breakfast if you want."

The Dodgers won the Series on the playing field, four games to two. Veeck won with ease on style and grace and warmth.

"O'Malley," he later remarked, "has the kind of face that even Dale Carnegie would want to punch."

Like all lusty smokers Veeck coughed, but presently his coughing spells grew longer and more violent. They built and built and built until he fainted. He developed persistent headaches and physicians suspected lung cancer which had metastasized. Veeck read volumes on cancer and suspected the same thing. He and Mary Frances were raising six children, none older than twelve. With neither complaint nor panic, he sold the White Sox in 1961, to put his finances in proper order for his heirs.

He was not suffering from lung cancer. Specialists at the Mayo Clinic discovered that a blood vessel near his brain had weakened. Bursts of coughing made the artery balloon. The effect was similar to what happens when a man takes a ferocious blow to the head. Concussion and unconsciousness. The treatment was simple. Lead a quiet life. Then the weakened blood vessel would have a chance to strengthen itself, as, indeed, it did.

On Maryland's Eastern Shore, Veeck found a rolling spread of houses, shingled barns and great rooted trees beside a dirt road called Tranquillity Lane. His front lawn sloped toward a quiet estuary called Peachblossom Creek. There he set about gardening and fathering and, when his health returned, bidding for major league franchises.

I visited him as often as I could. He is a proud man, but you could tell that he felt exiled. He had made important enemies, with his ebullient style and his dogged irreverence toward all the lords of baseball, including William Veeck. He was not a magnate, he said, but a hustler, same as everybody else who owned a ball club. Baseball was a lovely game, but without it the country would survive. Ultimately, it was entertainment, just like the circus. Most other owners were pompous anachronisms. If they ran Congress, Kansas and Nebraska would still be trying to get into the Union. "With all the enemies he keeps making," someone remarked in 1965, "baseball will let Veeck back in the day the Klan decides to welcome Jackie Robinson."

Curiously, as Veeck himself put it, whenever he tried to buy a team, his offer came up short. Even extravagant offers were rejected. The only evidence of a blacklist was existential. Bill Veeck, who broke attendance records in Milwaukee and Cleveland and Chicago, could not buy his way back into baseball with a check drawn on the Federal Reserve.

"Have you tried your American Express Card?" I asked.

His smile was bittersweet. "I've even offered to pawn the kids," he said.

Visiting him in Maryland, one was at first put off. The large living room, decorated with Navaho rugs and casual open furniture, rang to the sound of television. Old movies. Game shows. The Galloping Gourmet. Frances, a gracious, attractive, organized brunette, would steward my wife and children to the guest house. Veeck's older boys, Mike and Gregory, helped with the luggage.

The major-domo sat on the couch in shorts, reading. He was always reading. Sometimes as he read, two or three books lay open at the same time. War histories, novels, spy stories, political essays, even baseball books, and he read so rapidly that sometimes his speed surpassed his pronunciation. To this day, he calls the tranquilizer that deformed babies "Tamilodide."

His greeting was offhand. It took five hours to drive from New York to Easton, Maryland, which with the children seemed like a week, and Veeck's hello suggested that you had dropped by from next door.

He sipped a beer. He always sips beer, but drinks no whiskey. Then, reading two books, keeping a casual glance on the television, where Humphrey Bogart was making a sidelong move toward Mary Astor, he'd utter a startling statement—Franklin Roosevelt was a thief. As you answered, he'd turn more deeply to his books.

Partly this was style. Veeck likes to make you work to hold his attention. It was not rudeness. The chroniclers of Imperial Rome boasted that Julius Caesar was capable of doing seven things simultaneously. In the days of his idleness, Veeck was overcharged with adrenaline. He did three things at once because he had to.

"Roosevelt didn't steal. He had family money from boyhood," I announced.

Veeck looked up. On the television set, Bogart was telling Mary Astor that he had found her out. She was a killer. "What Roosevelt stole was Norman Thomas' platform," Veeck said. "He ran on a few old socialist ideas and called it the New Deal. Roosevelt became President with thoughts he took from Norman Thomas, and Thomas had to go and be a professor." On the big screen Mary Astor burst into tears.

I had been writing articles for the *Saturday Evening Post,* a magazine that several editors were dragging toward the twentieth century. "It may be working," Veeck said. "The stuff is getting pretty good. For the first time in years, people are stealing the *Post* out of my mailbox."

Some of our best friends were lawyers and doctors, but we agreed that if physicians did not end up with all the money in the United States, attorneys certainly would. "I'm thinking of dealing with that from within," Veeck said. "I'm starting to read for the law. That's what Lincoln did. You read and then if you can pass a bar examination you are licensed. There are only a few states where you can do that. Maryland is one."

"If you don't get back into baseball," I said.

"I made a splendid offer for the Washington Senators. There's a team that hasn't been promoted. You have Washington and all northern Virginia to draw from, and despite the politicians, there is a kind of glamour to the capital. I made a good offer. Keep a team in Washington. Why, it is even possible that you could keep Congressmen off your neck by giving free tickets to important committee chairmen. Not a bribe, of course. Congressmen do not accept bribes. Rather a gesture of good feeling from Ole Will, on behalf of the national pastime. I made my offer and the word from baseball was 'Close, but no.' Not 'No, thanks.' Just 'No.' They moved the Senators to Minneapolis, and now, when antitrust legislation has them scared to death, there's no ball club in Washington, no free tiokcts for important committee chairmen, no bribery. Beg pardon. No gestures of good feeling."

He sipped beer out of a can. "If this exile is permanent, I might even buy a bookstore. Then books would be my substitute for ball players."

Sitting opposite Veeck when he wore shorts, you noticed the artificial leg. For walking, the device was rigid, locked at the knee. When he sat, the leg extended like a plastic shillelagh. He turned a screw and the device bent 90 degrees and assumed the outlines of a normal leg when one is sitting.

Once he invited me to play tennis. He has imposing

hairy forearms and he hits a tennis ball hard. You could beat him by running him, of course. But then you were running a one-legged opponent. There was no middle ground. Hit the ball to Veeck and have him slam a rocket past you. Hit the ball away from him and live with your conscience. We rallied for a long time. I resisted his invitation to play a set.

Peachblossom Creek was wide and calm, a Maryland Moon River, lapping with the tides. Until jellyfish moved in each summer, the waters were irresistible, and we used to swim amid a shriek of children. Veeck unharnessed his artificial leg and moved through the water with a sturdy crawl. He likes children, his own and other people's. "Be ready," he warned one of my boys, who was four. "I'm coming after you and I'm a sea monster."

"I'm ready," the boy cried. "Come get me, sea monster. Come get me, you one-legged sea monster."

I blanched. Veeck didn't even blink. Then I remembered something he had written with Ed Linn, in *Veeck, as in Wreck.* "It has become customary in our euphemistic world to describe us cripples as handicapped. I'm not handicapped. I'm crippled. Webster defines handicapped as 'to be placed at a disadvantage.' I don't believe I'm there. I can do anything anybody else can do that doesn't involve sprints. So, far more important, though I am crippled, I am not handicapped."

Evenings, the talk grew more intense and turned toward baseball. He was devising new promotional plans, putting them into his files. No, he would not say what they were. Did he ask me to tell him my plots?

"When you get close to a team, Bill, can I throw $10,000 or $15,000 into your syndicate?"

"No help," Veeck said. "There are Federal rules governing the way I operate. I can't work with units that small." He sighed. "It probably doesn't matter anyway. These new syndicate-type fellers won't let me back in. I'm an individualist. In baseball today, that makes me as obsolete as Barnum."

To come back in December, 1975, he had to sprint through minefields. The syndicate-type fellers objected to his method of financing. They gave him a week to raise another $1.2 million in cash. When he succeeded, he won the oldest ball park in the majors and a burnt-out franchise. The White Sox he sold were profitable winners. The White Sox he bought fifteen years later had been losing for so long that the American League wanted to uproot the team to Seattle. (In a new setting, the first flash of major league baseball blinds locals to ineptitude. By emphasizing civic pride, by telling reporters that the city itself is on trial, by equating baseball attendance with respect for the National Anthem, you can draw with Snow White, eight clowns and one designated hitter.)

Veeck acquired the Sox on the Wednesday before a Friday trading deadline. Negotiations were completed in a suite at the Diplomat Hotel, a resort in Hollywood, Florida.

Veeck moved to the lobby, set up a chair and desk, under a sign that read, "WHITE SOX TRADING POST" and began making deals as rapidly as he could. The team he bought could hardly be worsened. Besides, trade head-

lines seldom hurt ticket sales. One owner snapped that
Veeck was impairing the dignity of the game. Smiling in
a dignified way, Veeck made six deals, involving twenty-
two players, within forty-eight hours.

He almost filled Comiskey Park for a game with Kansas
City opening day in the Bicentennial year. He drafted
Rudie Schaffer, his business manager, to wear a three-
cornered hat and play a snare drum. Paul Richards, his
field manager, donned a white wig and carried a flag.
Flanking them, in knee britches, his artificial shin naked
to the winds of spring, Veeck limped along, playing a fife.
The Spirit of '76 lasted long enough for the White Sox to
defeat Kansas City, 4 to 0, before 40,318 spectators.

That weekend cold weather struck. Then snow sprin-
kled Chicago. Opening-day momentum froze into inertia.
It was two weeks before the Sox played another home
game. On May 9, a line drive cracked the left knee cap of
Wilbur Wood, the Sox's most durable pitcher. Newspapers across the country ran photographs of Wood scream-
ing in agony. The season ahead was symbolized.

The new players Veeck acquired matched those he had
traded. Ralph Garr, an outfielder, who won a batting
championship in 1974, could not go back on a fly ball. A
variety of left fielders could not throw home. To para-
phrase, or blaspheme, Leo Tolstoy, all winning baseball
teams play defense in the same way. Well. Losers make
different kinds of mistakes. Eventually, in May, June, July
and August, the White Sox were going to make the single,
unique mistake that cost them the game.

That left Veeck's style and his promotions. He ripped

out his office doors and worked in public. He wanted the White Sox to be a quasi-public team. He answered his own phone and bantered with fans, growing sharp only when the fans tried to hustle a hustler. No, he was not interested in Cuba sugar investments or debentures guaranteed to pay 45 percent interest, or shares in a molybdenum mine that had not yet been dug in the Northwest Territories.

He sponsored scores of novelties, including music night. Anyone who brought an instrument and could play "Take Me Out to the Ball Game" was admitted for half-price. Two people arrived with pianos. Others brought tubas. Some thirteen thousand amateur musicians bought half-price tickets and they rose in the seventh inning and played their song, guided by the baton of an assistant conductor from the Chicago Symphony. The headless skeleton of Franz Joseph Haydn stirred in its Austrian grave. "But we invited no music critics," Veeck says, "and the next morning I got twenty calls from people who told me they'd never had more fun at a ball park. That's what you're supposed to have at a ball park. Fun."

In September he activated Saturnino Orestes Arrieta Armas Minoso, called Minnie and O. Restless Minoso by sportswriters when he starred for the White Sox twenty years before. Minoso, now fifty-three and one pound over his best playing weight, became the oldest man ever to bat in the major leagues.

"My reasoning was that it was a good promotion all by itself," Veeck says. "Besides, it is interesting to see this fifty-three-year-old man hustling down to first base on a pop fly. For some of our younger men, who are less enthusiastic, it made for an object lesson. One player objected to Minnie taking batting practice. That's understandable. You take Minnie at fifty-three hitting the ball into the left-field stands, and here's a guy of twenty-three who can't get the ball to the warning track. I'd want to bar him, too. Beyond all that, on the other hand I wanted Minnie to get a hit."

Minoso paused for an ovation on his first time at bat. He tipped his cap and waved. The cheers continued. Then he made out.

"Me no see ball," he explained to Veeck. "Tears."

In his sixth game as designated hitter, Minoso belted a major league fast ball on a low line to left field. He was now the oldest man ever to make a major league hit.

On this warm September evening two days later, the young pitcher Chris Knapp was throwing hard and holding his lead. Someone hit a drive toward right field, and Ralph Garr backed up a step and watched the ball bounce. It went for two bases.

"A hundred-dollar fine," I told Veeck.

"For what?"

"For a major league outfielder playing a fly like that."

"You're out of your time," Veeck said, impatiently. "A *thousand*-dollar fine wouldn't work with players today." He brightened when the Sox scored in the last of the eighth and won the first game, 4 to 3.

Charles O. Finley, the dapper, blunt Chicagoan who is the Emperor of the Oakland Athletics, arrived in the press box between games. Finley's white hair glistened in the kind of mane directors demand from central casting when they need an actor to portray a judge.

"Veeck," Finley said, "since you've activated Minoso and made a joke of the game, it's time for all us old men to activate ourselves. I'll activate me and you activate you."

Veeck nodded, but did not smile.

"You know the rules," Finley said. "No artificial aids. That means you gotta hit without your wooden leg."

"And you," Veeck said, "will have to bat without your hairpiece."

For the rest of the night Finley kept his distance.

The White Sox fell two runs behind in the second game, and a second baseman named Stein made two errors. "Are you caught in the salary boom?" I asked. "Do you have to pay these gentlemen much money?"

"You don't mind paying the good ones. The worrisome thing is the high cost of mediocrity. I'll give you an example, better in basketball because it's simpler. The Milwaukee Bucks started in the NBA with a lot of enthusiasm. They managed to lose $480,000, starting five guys named Joe. The next year they win the flip and they have Kareem Abdul-Jabbar. They pay him $200,000. They make $500,000. That's a turnaround of a million dollars. Obviously, Jabbar is worth what he gets. Now they double the salaries of the other four men who played with him. Next year they get Oscar Robertson for big money and they make a million and a quarter. The three original guys playing with Jabbar and Robertson get their salaries doubled again. They're playing just as lousy as they did in the beginning and now their salary has been quadrupled.

They simply rode up on Jabbar's and Robertson's shirt-tails.

"There's where your danger is. As the numbers for legitimate stars go up, they drag up players whose only claim to fame is that they can put on a uniform. You hit that all the time in baseball."

Back of center field, above the freshly painted empty seats, the scoreboard was silent. Going into the bottom of the eighth, Veeck's White Sox were losing, 4 to 2. Two men reached base. A beefy first baseman named Jim Spencer came to bat. Steve Mingori of Kansas City threw a slider and Spencer stroked it to right, not hard, nor even very high, but just hard enough and high enough to clear the railing in front of empty boxes. Three runs scored. The White Sox would win.

The scoreboard awoke. Explosions rang. Fireworks lit the South Side night. Mingori looked at his shoes and drew his spikes across the mound. Suddenly every loud-speaker at Comiskey Park erupted into the "Hallelujah Chorus" from the *Messiah*.

Mingori shifted his weight. The music rose. "Hallelujah, Hallelujah, Hal-le-lu-jah."

You are not supposed to root in a press box. You are supposed to be an emotionless observer and clinical. Unclinically, I clenched my right fist, lifted it shoulder-high and looked at Veeck. His last-place team was about to win a double-header.

"Hallelujah," I said.

Veeck winked. "It's supposed to be fun."

He left soon after the double victory, limping slowly

down the twisting catwalk on the roof of amiable ancient Comiskey Park. He saw me behind him, stopped, turned sideways and surveyed the cityscape to the south.

Nothing was there but street lamps. Even as I passed, I knew what he was doing. If we walked together, I would have to slow my pace to match his one-legged gait. Baseball's ebullient, hustling, wildest child is a sensitive man who does not like to impose.

He was going to finish last. In a world of syndicates for owners, among players tuned to the whims of business agents, it is possible he will not win another pennant. Even Branch Rickey finished his active days directing a last-place club.

But by September 25, hundreds of White Sox fans had organized a promotion of their own. Veeck *might* create a winner in two years. He had saved the White Sox from moving to Seattle. A game against Oakland was designated "Bill Veeck Appreciation Night."

In the season of his return, Veeck's luck held constant. It poured in Chicago on September 25. Bill Veeck Appreciation Night had to be canceled on account of rain.

7

The Great J.B.

Afterward, when autumn came, a cold, dry, naked autumn with withered leaves shuddering on branches, Wendy would refer to him as "your son." While I played baseball long ago in fields of dirt and rock, she learned dressage at Foxcroft, a school that instructed young ladies in the holy trinity of riding, Protestantism and virginity.

It was the spring of 1975 and I was wandering past a Florida dugout when Johnny Bench called my name. He was smiling and newly married and in love. We fell to easy banter.

"I wonder if you'll hit ten home runs this year. Walker Cooper used to say that no one was a pull hitter in the first year of marriage."

Bench looked serious and laughed with his eyes. *"That* isn't what uses up energy," he said. "It's the chasing. Now all I have to do is walk into the bedroom. We can even use the living room. No more chasing. I ought to hit more home runs than ever."

His face, under the broad brow, was free of lines. He stood, strong, happy, poised, in the fullness of his twenty-seven years.

"Where do you come from?" Wendy asked.

Bench assumed a farmboy's speech. "Binger, Oklahoma, ma'am."

"You'd better place it for her, John. She's more familiar with London."

"Binger," Bench said, "like finger, but with a 'b.' It's half a mile back of Resume Speed."

Wendy had wanted to take photographs at Al Lang Field, and I warned her that ball players in their dugouts say words that Miss Charlotte Haxell Nolan, the late chaste headmistress of Foxcroft, pretended did not exist. They said other words that Miss Nolan would not have believed existed if she had heard them. But here was Bench playing civilly with the language.

"Are you chewing gum?" Wendy said.

"Tobacco, ma'am."

"Could I try it?" Wendy said. "I've never chewed tobacco."

I walked off to say hello to Sparky Anderson, the retired car salesman who manages the Cincinnati Reds. Usually Wendy's face, under blond hair, glows with a subtle tawniness. When I returned to the dugout, green had invaded her complexion. Bench was observing and grinning wide. "It isn't fatal," he said. "It may not even require a stomach pump. I believe your wife has swallowed some tobacco juice. If you're a good husband, you'll take her to the press room and wash her stomach out with Scotch."

"What the hell happened, honey?" I said later.

"It was tobacco juice," she said. "But what could I do? Spit in front of all those young men? I swallowed." She made a sour face. She was recovering. "But I did enjoy meeting your friend Mr. Bench in the Cincinnati pit."

"Dugout," I cried, sounding like Jack Benny. "That's dugout."

"Baseball seems like a very complicated game," Wendy said, vaguely.

It was the autumn of the shuddering leaves. John Bench was older by one broken marriage. Amid the triumph of the Reds in 1976, his season was a failure. Slanderous gossip attended his separation. He had batted .234. He had heard boos. Sportswriters were suggesting that he was no longer the finest catcher in the game.

Bench works at nonchalance. Pride is what moves him. Now, mustering pride and discipline and concentration, he set out to make one October week his own. In the first game of the World Series, he loosed two throws that paralyzed the New York Yankees. They had won the pennant running. After seeing Bench's arm, they turned immobile as chess pieces. Batting with great skill that afternoon, Bench singled to center and tripled to right. He got another two hits in the second game and two more in the third. In Game Four he simply overpowered the ball and drove out two home runs.

The last home run, his eighth World Series hit, was an

enactment of the power hitter's art. He hit an outside slider—the pitch you're not supposed to pull in the first year of marriage, or while lawyers jockey you toward divorce, or even on the calmest of your days. As Wally Moon, Dixie Walker, Stan Musial or any other batting student explains, pulling a good slider produces a ground out. The pitch reaches home plate low and outside and literally slides farther down and away, from the batter. When you try to jerk the pitch to left field, you hit over the baseball, if you make contact at all. You tap it at the third baseman. One solution is turning on the ball. You turn your body and hit the ball early, actually before it reaches the plate. The ball is higher, closer then, and more accessible. The ball is also moving at eighty miles an hour. Your timing has to be exact.

Bench turned and timed the pitch perfectly and pulled the pitch toward left on a low, buzzing line and the ball rode and rode until it cleared the fence. He led the World Series in batting. He led the Series in home runs. His defensive play had been perfection. Once again Johnny Bench was the finest catcher in baseball.

"He's the best I've seen," I told Red Smith, "but I only go back to Berra and Campanella."

"He's the best I've seen," Smith said, "and I go back to Dickey and Cochrane."

Probably that makes Bench the best catcher since the beginning of baseball. In the locker room, he sipped champagne. He may have wept a little. He said he could not remember feeling better. He rode to the Park Sheraton Hotel in the team bus and walked into the lobby. He had no small jokes now, or nonchalance, or poise. His face was a glaze of joy and he looked very young, a large, triumphant child on Christmas morning when a soft, sled-riding snow has fallen and every present has been right. He was twenty-eight years old, and I wondered if he would ever know such happiness again.

Wendy had spent a summer watching ball games, often with an instructor at her side. She recognized what Bench had achieved. "Is that the way you'd wanted to play?" she asked me later.

"Like Bench in these four games? I didn't play that well even in dreams." I paused. "But it would be nice if one of my boys could play like that."

The mood was drifting toward sentimentality. "Your surrogate son," she said. "Johnny Bench is your surrogate son."

As most imagine it, a superstar lives a dream. He has fame and wealth and a kind of gliding happiness. He moves from victory to victory easily. He lives without strain. That is not the way things are for Bench. He played in the 1972 World Series, which the Reds lost to Oakland, with a lesion the size of a half-dollar on one lung. Across those seven games, his friend and lawyer Reuven Katz was checking the competence of thoracic surgeons. Bench was thinking, "I've never smoked. How can this be?" He made six hits, chatted genially with the press and signed the endless obligatory autographs. He kept his distress and his affliction to himself.

In Cincinnati now, Bench cannot shop, or bowl, or even

stroll without becoming the center of a crowd. People who have not met him feel they know him. You hear "Johnny, Johnny, Johnny," not "Mr. Bench." Others are competitive or hostile. "Hey, Johnny, how come you struck out twice last night?" Or, "Hey, Johnny, you're not so great. I think Thurman Munson is a better catcher." A superstar must plot to realize privacy, and unless he wants to live in a combat zone, he has to master the soft answer. "The pitcher has fine stuff. Munson? He's a fine ball player and the Yankees are winning."

Hustlers are forever approaching Bench with deals. "We've invented this car that can hit a brick wall at fifty miles an hour without injuring the occupants. It delivers fifty miles a gallon and it will last for at least ten years. We don't want any of your money, Johnny. We want you to accept a piece of the company and we'll give you the Ohio distributorship."

Around Cincinnati, Bench's name has signified excellence and credibility. People would *want* to buy a car from Johnny Bench. His baseball income will end when he reaches thirty-five, and he needs every solid investment he can find. But he has to sidestep promoters trying to use his name as a license for larceny. The car he was asked to sell does not exist. Its sponsors were going to use his name to secure orders and down payments. Then, pocketing the cash, they planned to fly off to some country that has no extradition treaty with the United States.

Bench, or rather Johnny Bench Enterprises, Inc., owns a major interest in a bank, and markets bats and balls and a water filter among other products. The gross including his baseball salary is said to approach $500,000 a year, which beats pulling cotton on the Oklahoma prairie. But success does not remove stresses. It only substitutes new ones for old.

I encountered Bench three times across the summer of 1976. At Dodger Stadium in May, I saw him walking toward the batting cage, and asked how things were going.

"Four lawyers," he said. "She's been to four lawyers and we could get everything settled if she just came and talked."

I'd been referring to his batting, which was erratic. Any lawyer representing Vickie Chesser Bench, a model pretty enough to have appeared on a toothpaste commercial, would find his nostrils flaring at the scent of money. The lawyer would want as much as he could get for his client and conceivably, just conceivably mind you, he might base his fee on the size of the settlement.

"And it just gets worse and worse?"

"It just gets worse and worse."

"Well, first of all everybody's divorce stories, yours and mine and Elizabeth Taylor's, bore the hell out of everybody else, unless they're scandalous. And second, people who go from lawyer to lawyer don't get more conciliatory. They get more adversarial. Try to get the damn thing over quickly."

Bench nodded and started to say something, but a stranger approached. Bench walked into the batting cage glumly and began to swing.

By the time I flew to Cincinnati, from Bill Veeck's ebullience with a last-place team in Chicago, the Reds were loping toward a pennant. Cincinnati rises among hills on the north bank of the Ohio River, a city of 500,000 where you can still see the country from downtown. It was an important river port, a railhead, and boosters refer to it as the Queen City.

In its past are *gemütlich* traditions of German immigrants, the founding of the first great center of Reform Judaism in America and generations of people called Taft. But by major league standards Cincinnati is a small town. The city, that part of it that one could see through baseball, was confident but not smug, as New York baseball people were smug when the Yankees dominated the game. Cincinnati people still protest, "We're number one." New Yorkers, in the days before their bonds went bad, had the same thought but no need to express it. In September John Bench, greatest of catchers, still had not gotten his divorce. He was not hitting home runs. His batting average had fallen fifty points from where it was the season before.

On the phone his voice rang with defiant cheer. "It's just an off year and some of the other guys on the team have picked things up. They've been fantastic. When we talk later, would you like to do it at a golf club? There's a good tournament going on and I have some friends on the tour."

I was staying at a motel south of the Ohio River in a place called Fort Mitchell, Kentucky. "I've got a rented car. I'll drive right over."

"I have some friends," Bench said. "None of them from baseball. I like to get away from baseball off the field. Be out front in twenty minutes and one of my friends will pick you up." Later someone would ask if Bench was being nice or simply working at public relations. Bench has gotten three million votes in balloting for the All-Star team. He is infinitely more sought after than seeking. Yes, he may have been working at his public relationship. He also is extraordinarily thoughtful.

The car was a metallic-gray Cadillac. The driver, a short, cheerful man of middle years, introduced himself as Herbie Goodman. "I sell ladies' ready-to-wear," he said. "There're four of us and we all have nicknames. Johnny calls me The Merchant Prince."

Bench owns a triplex condominium, overlooking the Ohio, which is no longer beautiful but somewhat less polluted than it was. Beyond the river rose wooded Kentucky hills. Bench was off on an errand and Herbie Goodman pointed out trophies, as proudly as though they were his own. Under glass in the living room, Bench had arranged a collection of Indian jewelry. Two nonrepresentational paintings hung on the walls. It was a quiet, tasteful, tidy home.

The door burst open and Catie Katz arrived. She is a warm and energetic lady, wife to Bench's lawyer, and she was on a legal mission. Opening cupboards and drawers, Catie took an inventory. "Vicki took some silver, but she seems to have left Johnny the Wedgwood dishes." More of the vitiating tedium of a divorce.

Bench appeared, in slacks and an open-collared shirt, an Indian pendant round his neck. He said it was going to be hot and changed to tennis shorts. He is a big, beautifully conditioned man, who stands six foot one and weighs about 215. His thighs are huge. Not fat but huge. He moves lightly, lithely, neither like a man so large nor like a catcher. His hands would fit a giant. When you greet Bench, you shake his hand. He shakes your hand, your forearm and your elbow.

Catie Katz continued her inventory and we moved to the gray Cadillac. "Do you think the divorce is affecting your hitting?" I said, as Bench drove down narrow streets toward an interstate highway.

"My left shoulder's been cramping," he said. "That's affected my swing. The shoulder is what's affected my hitting." He blocks the plate in an unyielding way, and on April 22, 1975, an outfielder named Gary Matthews dove into Bench's left shoulder as he tried to score. For the rest of the season, Bench had to play in pain. The cartilage at the top of the shoulder was so severely damaged that it had to be removed that November, and Dr. Donald O'Donoghue, the orthopedist, said "it looked as if the cartilage had been hit with a hammer." The operation was a success and the patient developed cramps. "I've been taking salt tablets," Bench said, "and the shoulder is feeling better. Besides, I'm having a good defensive year. If the divorce was affecting my hitting, wouldn't it also affect my catching?"

He was still having a good defensive year. Catching, even catching as well as Bench, is more mechanical than batting. Bench has that incredible arm. Not boasting, but simply stating a belief, he says, "I can throw hard enough and accurately enough to be a major league pitcher right now." He has native speed, "mobility" in the argot. Last year he stole sixteen bases in eighteen attempts. The heavy body, the enormous plowman's hands, move with incredible quickness. If you were to list specifications for an ideal catcher—size, reflexes, intelligence, the rest— you might exceed Johnny Bench, but only marginally.

Batting, it seems to me, is a more subtle skill. Ted Williams suggests that hitting a major league pitch is the most difficult single act in sport. That statement serves Ted Williams, the last man to bat .400 in the major leagues, but is convincing. A fine batter hits .300, that is he gets three hits for every ten times he comes to bat. More than two-thirds of the time, a fine batter makes out. Further, most hits come after a foul or two, or a miss. Perhaps the batter swings nine times for his three hits. Roughly then, the fine major league hitter swings successfully about one-tenth of the time. I cannot think of any other place in sport where one successful effort in ten equates with stardom.

To hit at all, you have to anticipate. Who is this pitcher? What kinds of pitches does he throw? What does he throw to *me?* What did he throw to me last turn at bat? Last game? Last month? Last year? What will he throw me now? Sportswriters call this "guessing," which Webster defines as reaching a conclusion without sufficient evidence. It is true that the batter cannot be certain what a pitcher is about to throw; batting is less precise an art than composing villanelles. But almost to a man, the better batters discipline themselves and make the most informed guesses. A clear mind helps that discipline. Extended divorce negotiations becloud the mind like hangovers. I suspect that without inventories of the Wedgwood Bench would have had a better season at the bat.

We had reached an interstate. Bench flicked on his CB radio. "Breaker 19," he said. "This is Sidewinder. A smoky report northbound to Kings Island, please."

"You're clean and green all the way, Sidewinder," a voice drawled, and Bench pushed the Cadillac faster.

"We all have nicknames," Herbie Goodman said. "I'm The Merchant Prince. Johnny is Sidewinder."

"Moving from one light topic to another," I said, "can we go from divorce to your lung surgery?"

"What do you do for heavy stuff back in New York?" Bench said. He grinned. "Look, I've got a Jew for a lawyer and a Chicano for a lung surgeon. How can I get into trouble?"

"Johnny likes the ethnic jokes," Goodman said.

"What do you get," Bench said, "when you mix a Polack with a Jew?"

I didn't know.

"You get a janitor," Bench said. "But he owns the building."

It should be superfluous to point out that Bench tells his ethnics with the lightness one finds in people who are free of prejudice. He is himself one-eighth Choctaw Indian. Brooks Lawrence of the Reds front office, a black who pitched for St. Louis when baseball racism raged loud and ugly, marvels at the way Bench works with young black pitchers. Bench tells ethnic jokes for a single reason. He thinks they're funny.

"There's a lot of new technical work being done in lung

surgery," Bench said. "Staples instead of stitches." He had witnessed a number of lung operations after his own, and described them in clinical detail. "I feel pretty strongly about smoking now," he said. "I head the athletes' division of the American Cancer Society."

The Cadillac rolled quietly past small Ohio farms. "I had this routine chest X-ray in 1972," Bench said, "as part of the physical the team puts us through. Someone from the hospital called me and said they wanted to take another. The first was blurred. I went back. Then they wanted a third, a graph X-ray. Just routine, they told me. After that they wanted some more, still just routine, according to the nurse.

"I asked her what was wrong. She told me nothing was wrong.

"I said I wouldn't go along with any more of this. I wouldn't hold her responsible, but unless she told me what was going on, I wouldn't let them X-ray me again. That's when I found out about the lesion."

Reuven Katz is not only attorney for Bench, but also represents the surgical department of the University of Cincinnati Medical School. Going over rosters of surgeons, he settled on Dr. Luis Gonzalez, who moved to Cincinnati from Mercedes, a hamlet in the plains of southern Texas.

Bench accepted Katz's choice and found Gonzalez both professional and likable. On the morning of the operation for what might have been a fatal lung cancer, Gonzalez appeared to reassure his patient. Bench showed neither fear nor reverence. "Hello, Wetback," he said.

Within, he was trying to come to terms with what had happened. "I accepted the fact that my baseball career might be over," he said. "I was twenty-six, but it had been a good career. I'd done everything but played on a winning World Series team. All right. I wasn't just a ball player. I had a mind. I was valedictorian in my class at Binger High School. Now when you write that, please don't point out that there were only twenty-one in the class. Anyway, I was lucky. The lesion was benign."

"You weren't thinking about death?"

"I honestly wasn't. Just that I might never play ball again."

"That can be a kind of death," I said.

"Maybe it was for the Boys of Summer. But I'm not just a Boy of Summer and neither are you."

Bench slowed, turned off to the Kings Island Country Club, and proceeded past signs directing cars to distant lots. "We're going to park close to the clubhouse," Bench said, "but there's a cop up there. How will we get past him?"

"Use my name," I said.

A jackbooted state trooper raised both hands and tramped toward the car. "Members only," he began, then saw Bench and his jaw fell open. "Park anywhere you want, Johnny," he said.

We drove to a lawn beside the clubhouse. "You didn't use my name," I said to Bench.

"Saving it for an emergency," Bench said.

Bench parked and began walking the course. The other members of the Cincinnati Quartet appeared. Cadillac

Charlie is Charles Shanks, a lean, intense engineer with General Motors. Squirrel is James Staatmiller, an advertising salesman for radio station WSAI, who bounces when he walks. Sidewinder, The Merchant Prince, Cadillac Charlie and Squirrel wandered off to find who was leading the tournament.

Bench chatted with Jack Nicklaus and Miller Barber. He applauded good shots and silenced talkers around the greens. It was a brilliant, sunlit morning. He was stopped two dozen times for autographs. "Pace too fast for you?" he asked. "If I can walk and write, you ought to be able to do the same." Three hostesses approached, each with her name printed on a badge that was pinned to the left side of her blouse. "Please sign our badges, Johnny," a pretty brunette said. She offered a pen.

Bench signed, the huge left hand first lifting the badge and almost, but not quite, making contact with a breast. He walked on unsmiling.

"You've got a great pair of hands, Bench," I said.

"Yeah," he said. "Thirty-four C."

The Dodgers were in Cincinnati, but the pennant race was dead. The Reds played very well, but the games lacked excitement. "Imagine," Vince Scully, the Dodger broadcaster, said. "Going from these three to a double-header in Atlanta. *Atlanta.* They had a jacket night. The first 7,500 people would get an Atlanta jacket free. Only about 4,000 showed up. I've got to get off the road." Scully brightened. "But while I'm there would you like me to get you an Atlanta jacket wholesale?"

"Do you have enough for your chapter?" Bench said.

"Except for the World Series," I said.

The Cincinnati press box is air-conditioned and sound-proof. You cannot hear crowd noises or bat hitting ball or ball thumping glove. The game, beyond the glassed-in sportswriters, is a dumb show. You see the players moving in silence, as if the Astroturf of Riverfront Stadium were a huge television backdrop and someone had turned off the sound.

I moved to sit with Scully in fresh air. Herbie Goodman, The Merchant Prince, found me. "Johnny thought you might want this." He handed me a baseball. After a day of autographing Bench had inscribed it to me, writing, "We're not all Boys of Summer!"

I have a number of signed baseballs. This one sits alone on the mantel within a bell jar. It is not there because of the inscription. It is there because it was offered. I did not have to ask.

On Friday, October 15, the night before the World Series began, Dr. Luis Gonzalez held a party for twenty people in his pleasant, rambling home on Erie Avenue. The menu was a rousing combination of frijoles, tacos and enchiladas. Six old Chicano friends, visiting Cincinnati for the Series, had been invited, along with Reuven and Catie Katz. The star guest was John Bench.

Luis Gonzalez is trim, dark-haired, proud of his rise from dusty Texas, proud of his family, proud of his heritage.

"Rogelio," he greeted me. "You are welcome, Rogelio." Luis Mayoral, Clemente's friend, had called me Rogelio in

Puerto Rico months before. "Meet our guests," Luis Gonzalez said. "This is The Sheriff." He indicated a large, smiling man, who sipped a Margarita. "Next to him is The Godfather. We knew each other long ago in Texas. Excuse me briefly. I'm about to win a game of pool from Mr. Bench."

The two played solemnly in a festive room and split two games. Then The Sheriff wanted to tell a story about Bench. "We took him shooting in Texas and he hit a deer, but not where he was aiming. He hit the deer in the hindquarters. Someone else finally made the right shot and I explained to Johnny that we have a man in Texas who makes special trophies. He does not mount deer heads. He mounts deer asses. We would have had the trophy made, but Johnny said he could not accept it."

Bench laughed and said quietly, "You see how uptight I am." If you are truly relaxed, I thought, you do not protest. It was World Series eve and Bench's entire season had come down to his performance across a single week.

Riverfront Stadium was sold out on a summery Saturday afternoon, and fans wore buttons that read, "We're Reds Hot." In the huge parking garages people sat on the tailgates of station wagons and joked and gobbled sandwiches and drank martinis.

In the second inning of Game One, Lou Piniella, the Yankees' designated hitter, lined a double to right and moved to third base when Chris Chambliss grounded out. Piniella is not fast. He took a modest lead. Bench and Pete Rose have a signal for a pick-off play. The signal flashed. Bench fired from his crouch. The throw was like a major league fast ball. Piniella was safe, but narrowly. Now the Yankees had seen the arm of Johnny Bench.

In the sixth inning, Mickey Rivers, who had stolen forty-three bases for the Yankees, broke for second. Bench cocked his arm. Joe Morgan was slow in covering the base. Waiting, Bench pumped and pumped again. Then he fired into Morgan's glove and the fastest Yankee base runner was out by a foot. Now the Yankees had seen not only the arm but Bench's poise. Billy Martin, their manager, reacted with awe, or terror. He did not challenge Bench again until the World Series was lost.

Respecting Bench's power, the Yankees pitched him outside. Bench stroked one slider on the ground through the middle and slashed another off the wall in right for three bases. The game was quick, decisive and routine. The Reds won, 4 to 1.

That evening Reuven and Catie Katz threw an elegant party. They hung a banner—again "We're Reds Hot"— above their doorway and installed floodlights to play on it. They hired a pianist, who warmed up with Liszt and Chopin, and bartenders and chefs who mixed omelets to your order.

Bench was there early. Cadillac Charlie, Squirrel and The Merchant Prince arrived. Rawlings Jackson Eastwick III, a Cincinnati relief pitcher, who answers to "Rawley," brought his parents. He didn't throw a curve ball, Eastwick said, with the hubris of twenty-five years, and didn't have to because his hard stuff was so fast. His father, who works for Bell Telephone, looked pained. Approaching sixty, Mr. Eastwick was completing work toward his baccalaureate at Rutgers. He had always wanted a college degree and now he was going to have one. Shyly, the venerable undergraduate showed me a ring. "That's the night-school equivalent of a Phi Beta Kappa key," he said.

Perez chattered with his wife in Spanish until Reuven Katz said, "Come on, Tony. Don't exclude everybody from your conversation."

Perez explained that he knew he might be traded after the Series, but whatever happened, his years in Cincinnati had been happy. He is six foot two, a darkly handsome Cuban.

"God," Wendy said. "They're all a foot taller out of uniform."

I sat with Sparky Anderson, a trim man of forty-two, whose hair is white and whose face bears the lines of a scrambling life. Anderson was a journeyman infielder, never good enough for the major leagues, and now he was managing the best ball club on earth. I asked him about selling cars in the smog of Van Nuys, California.

"I hated it," he said. "People think that car salesmen are cheats, but the biggest cheats are the public. There are these tricks. Lowballing. You tell a customer that he can have a car for less than it cost you, but first you want him to check around with three other dealers. Of course no one else matches the price. So he comes back. Then you add on extras. Your price goes up enough to make a profit. But the customer is tired of dealing. He takes your offer, maybe complaining, but he takes it. I didn't like the business, but who's really doing the cheating? The salesman who's lowballing, or the customer who tries to get something for less than cost?"

"Both," I said.

"I hated it," Anderson said, "and all I could make was $7,500 a year. When I got an offer to manage Rock Hill in the Western Carolinas League, I took it before I even looked at a map to see where Rock Hill was."

He won a pennant at Rock Hill and at St. Petersburg and at Modesto, California, and at Asheville, North Carolina, and he has won four in his six seasons at Cincinnati. But when he talked about lowballing in Van Nuys, you could see that those days haunt him. He did not want to sell automobiles any more.

"It must be complicated running the Reds," I said. "All those stars and all those egos."

"You're damn right," Anderson said. "We're a team, but we have to take the egos into account. Use them. Joe Morgan runs the base-running for me in spring training. Bench runs the pitching. I'm fortunate to have leaders, but I'm not afraid to let the leaders lead."

"Do you enforce curfews?"

"For Pete Rose? For Joe Morgan?" He shook his head. "No. But I do have curfews for the kids. I come right out in spring training and I tell them that there are three Hall-of-Famers on the Reds [Bench, Morgan and Rose]. They aren't all going to be treated equally because they aren't all equals. If they want equality, play somewhere else. They won't find it on the Cincinnati Reds."

Bench sat beside the piano, comfortable with the game he had played, singing country-Western songs in a soft, tuneful baritone. He seemed happy, but all the songs were sad. One told of a lonely man who found comfort only in old dogs, children and watermelon wine. Another described a high school class and its dream of changing the world. But someone worked as a hairdresser and someone sold real estate and someone was bankrupt and someone had stolen a friend's wife and someone else had gone insane and the world was the same world yet, brightened merely by the memory of dreams.

"Here's one that's a little personal," Bench said. The song described a love that had gone wrong. It was over. That was all the couple knew. It was over. There was nothing left but to find the reason why. And still the couple couldn't say goodbye. Was that really personal? Or was he acting? And did he know? Then other people sang lively, bouncing numbers.

By the next day the weather turned around. The Sunday game was played at night, to better the ratings of the National Broadcasting Company, and the evening broke raw and wintry. The only person in the stands who did not wear a coat was Bowie Kuhn, the Commissioner of Baseball, who had acceded to the NBC request and was going to show all of us that damnit, it wasn't really cold. Kuhn sat in a sports jacket, prompting speculation that deep beneath, he wore long thermal underwear.

The best game of the Series was played in that cold. More confident now, Bench pulled a double to left and singled. Catfish Hunter, who pitched for the Yankees, was wild, but Hunter is a competitor. With guile and guts, he reached the ninth inning with the teams tied. I had been wandering among the bundled customers, but by the ninth I found a seat in a heated box beside Stan Musial. Ken Griffey, a speedy Cincinnati outfielder, reached second when the Yankee shortstop threw away his grounder. Hunter deliberately walked Joe Morgan. Tony Perez was the hitter.

"No matter how many Series I see," I said to Musial, "I still get butterflies in a situation like this. You?"

"Nah," Musial said. "Cincinnati's gonna win."

Perez lined Hunter's first pitch safely into left field. Cincinnati 4; New York 3. Musial nodded.

The Series moved to New York and the Reds won the third game, as they had won the first, routinely, this time by 6 to 2, Bench pumping out two more hits. Afterward it was our turn to take him out in New York. I chose the 21 Club because I had never seen a celebrity interrupted there at dinner for an autograph.

Bench talked about playing in the cold. Reuven Katz asked if he was satisfied with his two hits that night and he said, no, that he had wanted a third, and that every hit was important because it would be nice to set a record for most hits in a World Series.

"With those throws in the first game," I said, "especially the one to third, were you trying to intimidate the Yankees?"

"There is an intimidation factor in baseball," Bench said.

"Let's let him up," Katz said. "He's had enough baseball for today."

When we were eating, a bus boy timorously extended a pad and pen to Bench. He put down his fork and signed. The waiter asked next. Then a captain and suddenly people were lining up. Bench signed and cut his steak and signed and lifted a fork and signed and chewed and signed and swallowed.

Finally, a lady announced that she had four children back home.

"That's your problem," Bench said.

"And I need autographs for all of them. Gwen is seventeen and Billy is twelve and playing Little League. He's fast and he's an outfielder and—"

"Lady," Bench said, "if you will stop talking, I will sign." Before he could finish his steak, it was as cold as a Sunday night in Cincinnati.

In the fourth game, Bench hit a towering homer down the left-field line, putting the Reds ahead by two runs. The second homer, in the ninth inning, batted in three. The Reds won, 7 to 2, the five runs supplied by Bench making the difference. It would be reaching to say that Bench, all by himself, was the difference in the Series. The Reds were a better ball club than the Yankees. But short Series are not always decided on form; it would not be reaching very far.

On a television monitor one of the sportscasters said that next week at this time NBC would present a dramatization of *Captains and the Kings,* a title Taylor Caldwell reached by slightly misquoting Kipling. In the *New York Times* a few days later Red Smith described the Series as forgettable.

That depended on where one sat. From a distance, watching a great Cincinnati ball club sweep the Yankees, one could remark, as Jimmy Cannon did once, that the losers "should have paid their way into the ball park."

Beside Bench, seeing him salvage his season and wrest his career from decline—and his face, his face frozen into inexpressible joy—it was a Series quite beyond forgetting.

My voyagings were done and there would not be any baseball any more. Its revels now were ended, and I remembered in the autumn cold my son—not Johnny Bench, but Roger—playing at baseball in just as cold a spring amid the casual prosperity of Westchester County.

I telephoned the boy. "How did you like Bench?"

"Like him? I hate him."

"How can you hate a great ball player?"

"You know how I root, Dad. I hate him because he's not a Yankee."

Roger will hate Johnny Bench until he meets him. Then *his* face will freeze in joy, and Bench being Bench may invite Roger to play a game of catch.

But that is for another season in the sun.

Epilogue
After a Chilly Autumn

The Northeastern states went directly from summer to winter, without the benediction of an autumn. Of all climates, I like the first cold northwest winds the least. October is the cruelest month.

A man resists season change as he resists the passage of time. Nothing is stable. All is in flux. And one grows older. Today is the first day of winter, and all summers, even last summer, are locked into history with Tyre.

Wally Moon is not at John Brown University today. He is in Florida, during a classroom break, instructing young men at a baseball school. Recently he bought a franchise in the Double-A Texas League and next year, he says, he will be "semiactive" as president of the San Antonio Dodgers. His son Wally Joe, the free-form poet, will work there daily as assistant general manager.

Moon will continue to coach and teach at John Brown. His Golden Eagles were eliminated by Kentucky State in the semifinal round of the NAIA Region V Championships. Two of Moon's collegians, Chuck Gardner, the shortstop, and outfielder Randy Rouse, were drafted by Houston. They are trying to work their way up through low minor leagues. John Brown's team finished the season with a record of 37-and-5, and a team batting average of .362. Moon expects to have another good ball club next season.

After the Los Angeles Dodgers dropped out of the race and finished second, a league behind the Reds, Walter Alston's tenure as manager ended at twenty-two years. In the official announcement, Alston, who spoke so fondly of his "delightful job," decided to retire. Other sources say that retirement was suggested to him by people in the Dodger executive offices. Tom Lasorda, whose veins course with blood of Dodger royal blue, is the new manager. As a younger man, he will be closer to his players than Alston was; how good those players are going to be is the question.

Vince Scully, so weary of the road after a quarter-century of baseball travel, has moved to change the nature of his life. He signed a contract with CBS Sports, and he will continue to broadcast Los Angeles games, but only those at Dodger Stadium. The CBS travel, more short trips and no long ones, seems to him "a more sensible way for a family man to live."

As Bill Virdon foretold, the Houston Astros played better baseball in 1976. They finished third, just two games under .500, became the second most improved team in the major leagues. Still their attendance remained under 900,000. When no outsider could be found who would meet the asking price for the Astros, the various credit companies running the team assumed ownership. The practical effect can scarcely be encouraging; it is hard to imagine the General Electric Credit Corporation as an inspired owner.

There are no Berkshire Brewers any longer. The town of Pittsfield, Massachusetts, has appropriated $100,000 to refurbish old Wahconah Stadium. While construction proceeds, Pittsfield has no ball park and thus no team. After their good beginning the Brewers slumped, but two played in the major leagues last September. Jim Gantner filled in at third base for Milwaukee; Danny Thomas, who struck the umpire in the Eastern League, played thirty-two games for Milwaukee, batted .276 and hit four home runs. As an embryo major leaguer he now wants to be called Dan Thomas, so that he will not be confused with the comedian.

West Haven, a Yankee farm, won the Eastern League play-off, sweeping three games from Three Rivers, which is affiliated with Cincinnati. The winners' share for the World Series was approximately $27,000 a man. For winning the Eastern League play-off, each West Haven Yankee received a check for $15.70.

Leo Durocher was not asked to manage Seattle; Darrell Johnson was hired to manage the new team. That effectively killed Artie Wilson's dream of returning to the big leagues. He still sells cars in Portland, Oregon.

A wire service has reported that Stan Musial was going to leave St. Louis and buy the Cleveland Indians. Denying the story, Musial commented on both the American economy and the reckless expansion of the major leagues. "Now is not the time to buy a ball club," Musial said.

Despite expansion no one in baseball has hired Early Wynn. He continues to be the only Hall-of-Fame boat salesman of my acquaintance.

Progress on Ciudad Deportiva, the memorial to Roberto Clemente near San Juan, has consumed most of a $667,000 capital fund. Slow as that progress is, Mrs. Vera Clemente talks hopefully of support in Congress for an appropriation to finish the job. "But," she says, "getting everything done will take the next ten years."

After the White Sox finished last, Bill Veeck began negotiating with the State Department for a trip to Cuba, where he intended to sign talent across the sugar-cane curtain. Veeck's thirty-second operation—this time to relieve pressure on the cervical spine—intervened. Veeck had three phones installed in his room at Illinois Masonic Hospital and honed his biting humor. "Next season," he said, "they have us opening against the Toronto Blue Jays. How's that for a natural rivalry? The White Sox, a charter American League club, at Toronto? But we have a chance to win, if we can get there. If necessary, I intend to lease dog sleds."

Johnny Bench appeared on the Johnny Carson show, where Shelley Winters seemed to proposition him on camera. Bench was gallant enough to keep his biting humor under control. This was the winter he had looked forward to, a winter of reflecting on triumph and enjoying his ease.

Roger has forsaken baseball for hockey. One night,

wearing the colors of the All Around Travel Agency, a suburban response to Les Canadiens, he scored three goals, and two more the following afternoon. As we approached the rink the next morning, another twelve-year-old asked if he had really turned the hat trick. Roger's response was an impatient "Yup." Baseball still held me. I turned to him and said, "Please. Try to win like Bench, not like Mantle."

"Yup," Roger said, impatiently.

As for myself, I shall remember the baseball summer of 1976 above all the others I have known.